YOUR SUCCESS

Angelos Sanders & Mo Haykir

ISBN: 978-1-5272-2906-8

First published 2018

Disclaimer

The boring (but necessary) bit...

This book not only gives you the theory behind success, but also actionable, practical ways to bring the theory into the real world and start making a difference in your life. However, we have been told that we need to include the below disclaimer:

Our intent is to offer general guidance, to help support your life and career. It is not a substitute for any medical, professional, or career related advice. No responsibility for loss or damage occasioned by any person acting, or refraining from action, as a result of the material in this publication can be accepted by the authors. The information within this guide does not represent the views of any third-party service or organisation. Any use of this information is at the reader's own discretion and at their own risk. Neither the publisher nor authors accept responsibility for any damage, loss or claim, because of the use, or misuse, of the information included in this publication. No responsibility will be accepted by the authors or publisher for materials provided by third parties, including websites.

Now that's out of the way, we can get on with the book!

About the Authors: Angelos and Mo

Hello and welcome! Thank you for buying this book and making a commitment to achieving your success.

We are extremely proud to share this book with the world and know that it contains information that can help people achieve their success and unlock their true potential.

Our introduction in the next chapter goes into the detail as to why we wrote this book, who the book is for, how to use the book, and our promise to you.

Why We Are Qualified to Write About Success

We have both been on an entrepreneurial and personal development journey and have had significant levels of success at a relatively young age. We host a weekly podcast called Your Success Podcast (www.yoursuccesspodcast.com). On the podcast, we provide actionable insight into real life accomplishment through interviews with highly successful people from a variety of industries and backgrounds.

We have interviewed people from the worlds of business, property, law, media, personal development, sports, the military, and even Guinness World Record Holders – altogether we have accessed a total of **over 1,700 years of collective experience!**

It is the combination of wisdom from these interviews, our own personal experience from our journeys, and research into personal development and mindset over the past 10 years, that has enabled us to distil this information into **The 10 Key Traits of Success** – all of which you will learn about in this book.

We have learnt many lessons on our journey to success, through starting multiple successful businesses and enduring failures along the way. All of these experiences have helped us grow. However, we believe that you can fast-track your path to achievement by learning and implementing The 10 Key Traits of Success.

Before we begin and to help you get to know us, here's a short biography detailing our success journeys so far.

Angelos

Greetings reader! I'll start with a little bit about me. So, sit back, relax, and enjoy!

I am the son of a Greek Cypriot immigrant mother and English father, born and raised in Plymouth, (England, UK). My parents never had much money, but what they lacked in cash they made up with love and support. At a young age, I realised that my parents were struggling to afford to feed myself and my brother. That realisation stuck with me and that is why, ever since then, I have been determined to be the best that I can be in life.

I was very mischievous at school. I had so much energy within me and struggled to focus the energy positively. However, I still managed to make a Batmobile go-kart for my graded school project, of which I was very proud.

My first ever job was working for an elderly lady, cleaning weeds from her driveway for 50 pence an afternoon; even at the age of 7, I knew she had me on the cheap (coincidentally, I now own the very same house that I used to remove weeds from!).

At age 15, my next part time job was working at my uncle's fish and chip shop most weekends, which was really good fun. I had to be very fast at washing dishes as the hot water tap poured out water as hot as lava, so I became very efficient at it! I fondly remember having finished my first ever shift in the early hours of the morning. In my excitement at making a step towards success, I realised that I didn't have my house keys on me. I rang my parent's doorbell but there was no waking them. So, I had to settle for sleeping on the porch with a doormat for a pillow. Who says the life of an entrepreneur isn't glamourous?

To the City...

I couldn't wait to leave school behind and enter the world of work. At age 16, the opportunity arose to work in a bank in the City of London and I embraced the adventure with open arms. I promptly packed my bags and moved to the big city. I was fed up with being bound by the rules of the classroom and learning subjects which I didn't believe were going to help me in the real world.

Working and living in London meant I had to grow up quickly, especially considering that I was responsible for authorising and then sending hundreds of millions of dollars around the globe on a daily basis! I lived alone, which wasn't easy, but you soon adapt to your new surroundings and meet new people – some of whom I am proud to call my friends to this day.

The biggest lesson I learnt from working in London for those three years was how to become independent and self-reliant. Both skills greatly helped me later on at university, then into the corporate world, and later in the world of business and entrepreneurship. It also made me impatient to succeed.

Upon returning to Plymouth from London, I applied for a part time job at a local bank to help supplement my income as a university student. However, I soon realised that my interview technique wasn't as polished as it should have been. I was waiting for the bank manager to arrive and I sat there nervously, checking my watch as I noticed that she was five minutes late. I thought, "this isn't very professional". Another five minutes passed. "What kind of place is this?" I wondered.

A whole 15 minutes passed, and when the manager arrived, I wasn't overly impressed. I mentioned at the start of the interview that I didn't really appreciate being kept waiting. Needless to say, the interview didn't last too long, and yes curious reader, I was not offered the position. I took solace in the fact that they sent me a letter, saying that they would keep me on file should another role arise in the next six months – most kind. The lesson here is not to criticise the time-keeping skills of the person you are looking to be employed by!

Studying Computer Systems & Networking at university was as you can imagine quite academic, but I felt it was a step backwards for me, as I had already worked in industry and I just wanted to be out there making money and not studying. However, I realised that to progress in the world of computing, it was important to have some kind of formal education.

The modules that I enjoyed most were the business and entrepreneurship ones; even then I knew where my real passion lay. Another benefit of the degree was the opportunity to undertake a placement year at an IT company looking after several production companies for Channel 4 Television. This was a real eye opener into the world of how TV shows are produced and great practical, on-the-job experience.

The Seed is Planted

Whilst it could be argued that my first real investment was in my education, the first tangible asset I bought was a six-bedroom student investment property in 2007. I was not particularly interested in buying a property or any other kind of asset at that time; all I wanted to do was climb the corporate ladder and become a director!

My mum practically had to force me to view the property, and I am very glad she did. Everything since then grew from that moment (thank you Panayiota). I saw that there was another way to make money rather than just working nine to five for someone else, I had caught the property bug and my eyes were opened!

The Book That Changed Everything

The year was 2009 and my investing had slowed down. The banks were reluctant to lend due to the 'credit crunch'. I wanted to invest in either highly profitable properties or make large sums of money by refurbishing run down, smelly old houses. I could not decide which I wanted to do, and it felt like I was in a car at the traffic lights: my foot was on the accelerator and the lights were green to go, tyres screeching, billowing smoke – but the handbrake was on. It was a very frustrating experience.

I was reading a property book by Dolf de Roos; his big plan and his amazing success made me realise that I also had to stop over-analysing which strategy to pursue and get out there and do it! Massive action had to be taken to get out of this 'chasing my tail' routine and so I took a week off work, viewed lots of properties, and bought two!

I realised the value of undertaking joint ventures (JVs), with friends and family initially, where I borrowed money from them and paid them a much higher interest rate than they could get from a bank. Fast forward to today: I have joint ventured with many people, raising close to a million pounds worth of JV funds. I continue to invest in property and other assets and have created significant portfolios.

Here are some quirky highlights from my property investing years:

- Digging (with my team) 50 tonnes worth of soil and stone by hand in the back garden of a property and carrying it through the house as there were no other exits to dispose of it!
- Completing four refurbishment projects at different properties in a single month!
- Owning an investment property with a Jacuzzi, which gained infamy (as you can imagine) as students would queue to have fun in the hot tub. The house got a reputation around the city, as well as on social media!

Whilst investing in property, I realised that it was quite a lonely journey with little support and even fewer people to bounce ideas off. I thought I would do something about it. I created the Professional Investment Group, affectionately known as PIG: a unique monthly network meeting where like-minded entrepreneurs converge to discuss property, business, and personal development, whilst also listening to experienced and influential guest speakers (www.pig.network).

I started PIG with seven people in my living room by the roaring fire. Now there are over 1,000 members across the south west of the UK. PIG has had many local, national, international, and even celebrity speakers present to the delight of audiences.

By the age of 31, I had left the corporate world behind once and for all. With the companies I had built up, I continued to grow both my property and events businesses full-time.

Never one to stay still for too long, I was thinking about starting a podcast focusing on property and business. At almost that exact time, Mo contacted me. I was on honeymoon, not with Mo, but with my beautiful wife. Mo asked whether I would consider starting a podcast – talk about synchronicity! And thus, Your Success Podcast (then known as PIG Pods) was born! I am really proud of the work that we have done to grow the podcast from nothing, to something that continues to inspire thousands of people around the globe on a weekly basis. Have a listen to our great interviews with amazing, inspirational people at **www.yoursuccesspodcast.com.**

Random facts about me:

- I love Star Trek with a passion and have a Twitter feed called "Just Star Trek" (juststartrek);
- I have participated in archaeological digs in Helike, Greece. Ancient Greek and Roman history are particular passions of mine;
- The Porsche 911 GT3 Turbo is my dream car.

You can follow my daily antics below:

Websites: www.angelossanders.com and www.pig.network

Facebook: Angelos Sanders

Instagram: angelossanders

Twitter: juststartrek

Hopefully this tale has not cured your insomnia, so I can now pass you onto the one and only Mo...

Mo

I was born in Turkey, and at the age of two came to the UK with my family. I grew up in the county of Essex (England, UK).

I've always had a strong work ethic and started work aged 15, in a local fish and chip shop, earning £2 an hour. What a weird coincidence that both Angelos and I started our careers in the fish and chip business! Even at the time, £2 per hour was a low wage. That said, it was much better than the £13 per week I used to earn doing a paper round in the pouring rain each day.

As an added bonus to the fish and chip shop work, I was given all of the leftover pies I could eat! They were still good after sitting in the warming cabinet for 14 hours, right? Anyway, I loved it: it put cash in my pocket and deep-fried food on tap. Plus, it was about a 30 second walk from where I lived.

As well as many other part time jobs, I also got involved with a few small business ventures (with varying levels of success). One such business I operated was a school tuck shop, which was set up as part of a young enterprise initiative and was hugely successful and profitable. It also meant that I was legitimately allowed to skip school to go the cash and carry to stock up on snacks and sweets. Sadly, we ended up winding the tuck shop down as theft of stock meant it wasn't viable to carry on. Who would have thought that leaving kids in charge of sweets would end in disaster?

This entrepreneurial spirit continued at university, where I ventured into running a marketing company – essentially acting as a South-West 'agent', employing staff and running operations for London-based marketing companies. I also co-founded a website called UniTextBooks.net, which let students buy and sell text books locally, rather than having to pay large amounts to post the (often very heavy) text books. However, to make this really work nationally, we realised we needed some serious cash to market to universities across the UK. We didn't have any serious cash at the time and didn't know how to raise it.

We also had an idea that we would sell advertising on the hand-stamps used to show that people had paid entry into a nightclub, and that allowed them entry back into the club if they went out for any reason. The only problem with this idea was that the sweaty nature of clubbing meant the hand-stamps smudged, so that any advertising would be completely unreadable. We toyed with the idea of using wristbands but in the end, we binned the idea.

It was during university that I started buying property, initially buying a student house with my now business partner, to renovate and live in during our final year. After graduating, we both went off to complete graduate training schemes: my business partner in construction, and myself in banking. We rented the property out and became student landlords.

We held on to our first property for a couple of years and then decided we needed to buy a bigger one, so we sold our first house on Moorview Terrace (which was the inspiration for the name of our company Moorview Property) and bought a slightly bigger house. What we didn't realise back then is that we could have refinanced our first house and kept it, and also purchased the second one.

So, we bought our bigger house, enlisted the help of a couple of friends to dig out the basement and do some minor works, and rented it out to students.

In 2014, whilst both still in full-time employment, we went along to a property education course and our eyes were opened to all of the opportunities available within property investing. What began with a conversation about not buying any of the education courses that were on offer ended with us signing up to almost everything, and starting a 12-month mentorship and accountability programme from January 2015! It was a fantastic experience, and by June 2015 my business partner had left his job to work on our property business full time, with me leaving my job in June 2016 to do the same.

Since then, we have bought many properties, and set up several six and seven-figure property and development businesses.

It is through property that I met Angelos, who had set up PIG (the Professional Investment Group) in Plymouth, where we first met. I then got involved in the launch of PIG Cornwall and went along to present at the first ever meeting in April 2017.

Since launching Your Success Podcast together, we have recorded episodes on everything: from vision and goal setting, to how to memorise Pi to 22,500 places, and have interviewed successful property developers, sportsmen, aspiring Hollywood actresses, and even a triple amputee Royal Marine who was wounded in Afghanistan.

Random facts about me:

- I used to teach windsurfing and run a bar in Egypt;
- I love hip hop and rap music;
- When I was in Secondary School, I wanted to be an Officer in the Royal Marines.

You can find out more about me here:

Website: www.mohaykir.com

Facebook: Mo Haykir

Instagram: muratjeffreyhaykir

Introduction

You have made a commitment to your success by not only buying this book, but also in the time you are going to spend learning and implementing its lessons.

Our promise to you is that once you have read and applied the wisdom in this book (utilising the tools in the toolkit) you will:

- ✓ Know **The 10 Key Traits of Success**;
- ✓ Have practical tools to be able to apply the traits;
- ✓ Believe that more is possible from life;
- ✓ Be able to overcome challenges;
- ✓ Plan and implement your vision of success.

What This Book Covers

This book details The 10 Key Traits of Success that we have identified from our own journeys, from our research over the past 10 years and through the interviews with successful people in Your Success Podcast.

A trait is a distinguishing characteristic that can be thought of as an attribute or feature. This is significant because there are common traits that appear in different successful people who come from a variety of backgrounds and careers. Not all successful people possess all traits, some possess one and others possess ten.

Therefore, the more traits you build into your own success journey, the greater the likelihood of success is.

1 Successful people define their vision of success.
2 Successful people are inspired by their vision and can self-motivate.
3 Successful people are constantly learning and growing.
4 Successful people are determined, and they persevere through challenges.
5 Successful people take ownership & responsibility for their life and do not live with regret.
6 Successful people do not let fear or limiting beliefs cripple them.
7 Successful people control their external environment.
8 Successful people are effective communicators, both internally & externally.
9 Successful people consistently take massive action.
10 Successful people maintain their traits consistently for long term success.
NATASHA

The 10 Key Traits of Success are:

1. Successful people define their vision of success.

Chapter 1 – You will learn the definition of success and how to define your own vision of success. There is no point starting a journey unless you know where you are going.

2. Successful people are inspired by their vision and can self-motivate.

Chapter 2 – You will learn how to draw inspiration from your vision and how to keep motivated, accountable, and find your flow.

3. Successful people are constantly learning and growing.

Chapter 3 – You will learn the importance of continuous improvement through education, having a growth mindset, and learning from failure.

4. Successful people are determined and they persevere through challenges.

Chapter 4 – You will learn how to overcome adversity, how to be adaptable, have patience, and consider long term vs short term thinking as well as the benefits of gratitude and perspective.

5. Successful people take ownership and responsibility for their life and do not live with regret.

Chapter 5 – You will learn why it is important to take ownership, about risk vs reward, living with no regrets, and eliminating excuses from your life.

6. Successful people do not let fear or limiting beliefs cripple them.

Chapter 6 – You will learn why fear exists and how to overcome both fear and limiting beliefs whilst giving yourself permission to succeed.

7. Successful people control their external environment.

Chapter 7 – You will learn about the impact that your external environment has on your likelihood of success as well as ways to enhance your environment by building your power team.

8. Successful people are effective communicators, both internally and externally.

Chapter 8 – You will learn how to effectively communicate with both yourself and other people, how to control your ego, and how to make a great first impression.

9. Successful people consistently take massive action.

Chapter 9 – You will learn the importance of taking sustained, massive action, as well as the importance of laser-like precision and focus to achieve your success.

10. Successful people maintain their traits consistently for long term success.

Chapter 10 – You will learn how to sustain long term success, avoid complacency, the importance of balance, and leaving a legacy to inspire future generations.

Due to the importance of each of the traits, each chapter is a deep-dive into one of the traits, with real life examples and action steps at the end of each chapter to help you put the learnings into practice.

Why We Wrote This Book

We wrote this book to help you achieve your vision of success, whatever that means to you, and to help you feel truly inspired in your day to day life. As we will explore in this book, many people's ideas of success are not actually their own ideas at all; they are the ideas pushed upon them by the media.

We also experience pressure from friends and family to:

- get a job that pays more;
- work for a big corporate company so that you get a good pension;
- choose what is safe and steady rather than taking risks and trying new things.

Our vision for the world is for people like yourself to have enough self-awareness to know what your own successful life looks like, and not to compare yourself to others. That doesn't mean not striving for huge, ambitious goals; it means knowing that what you are aiming for is truly what you want from life. Whether that is to make the world a better place, leave a legacy behind, or to build wealth, income or a business for your children, becoming a person of influence in your field, finding a cure for a disease, being the first person to set foot on a new planet, or simply having a lifestyle that means you can spend more time with friends and family: **this book will help you achieve this.**

Throughout the book, there are many examples from different areas of life and business, but The 10 Key Traits of Success are transferable. For example, where we mention business success, the traits that are required are the same for success in any field.

That's why this book is called YOUR SUCCESS!

That is truly what this book is about. Once you have finished reading and have completed the action steps at the end of each chapter, we know you will have a 'Your Success' plan and be ready to implement it.

The reference to 'hidden traits' on the cover is due to the fact that we only ever see the polished version of success and we do not see the underlying 'hidden' key traits that successful people possess. This is similar to the way we see a top athlete win the 100m race, but we don't see the months or years of gruelling, disciplined hard work and sacrifice that has gone into the training.

You will also notice that there are references to Ancient Greece and Rome throughout the book. These have been included to show you that the opportunities and problems, that we face today, have been experienced countless times, over many generations. Even with our modern technology and how far we think we have advanced, the human condition has remained fairly constant over millennia. The lessons learned from the past can still help us greatly today.

Who This Book Is For

This book is for anyone who wants to improve their life and become successful on their own terms. This book is for everyone who wants to be inspired and to make a difference in this world.

But there is a catch: you have to be prepared to put in the work. This book is not going to write that new CV. It's not going to formulate a business plan. It's not going to negotiate a new contract at work so that you can have more spare time to spend with your family.

It's also not for the quitters who stop at the first sign of trouble, or when things get a bit too much. This book is for positive people who look at failure or obstacles as the pathway to learning and greater success.

In summary, this book is for optimistic action takers and people wanting to be inspired by the journeys of other successful people.

The good news is that, even if you don't consider yourself to be an action taker or an overly positive person, you may well find something in this book to alter that. So please read on and let us know how you feel once you have finished reading – we feel confident that you will have experienced a change by the end of this book!

We have written this book together because we feel that our combined experiences and viewpoints will bring more value to you. We have tried to standardise the language and writing styles where possible, without losing our individual voices, to make it easier to read but you will still have the benefit of both of our insights into life and success.

How to Use This Book

This book can be used in many different ways. Much like everyone's idea of success is different, so too is their best way of learning. We have written this book so that you can:

- Read it cover-to-cover as a straight read,

or

- Use it as a reference guide, as each chapter is a stand-alone deep-dive into an individual success trait.

To get the most out of this book, we have created a companion Your Success Toolkit. It will serve as your guide to further expand on the action steps at the end of each chapter and to help accelerate your path to success. It can be downloaded at www.yoursuccesspodcast.com/toolkit

The toolkit is really where the rubber meets the road, and everything contained in this book starts to make a real change in your life.

Within the toolkit, we have compiled the ultimate resources designed to help you accelerate the path to your success, including examples of how we achieved success, templates, checklists, podcasts, YouTube videos, books and audiobooks.

At the end of each chapter, there is a set of action steps and the toolkit is where you will complete these to map out your success plan.

Keep in Touch

Our commitment to you is to help you every step of the way, to achieve whatever your vision of success is. To do this, we need to be able to stay in touch.

Join our mailing list via www.yoursuccesspodcast.com/inspireme to receive a regular dose of Your Success actionable inspiration and insight, and hear about exciting new releases of books and podcasts.

We would love to know your thoughts on this book and to hear about your success stories that have resulted from reading it so please reach out to us at hello@yoursuccesspodcast.com.

Let's Go and Do This!

To make it easier for you to implement the knowledge from each chapter, we have given you tasks to complete, which will transform the teachings into practical, life changing actions.

Chapter One is 'What is Success?', because Key Success Trait One is 'successful people define their vision of success'. Define success on YOUR terms and build a vision of the extraordinary life you have always wanted.

Every journey needs to have a clear destination and, by the end of Chapter One, you will have yours!

Table of Contents

Chapter 1

What is Success?

SUCCESS TRAIT 1:
Successful people define their vision of success

This chapter covers how to define success, since it's such a fluid concept that is very personal to each and every one of us, your definition of success is going to be different from someone else's, and as such you are free to create any vision of your success that you can imagine!

This chapter will give you a clearer understanding of what success is, introducing you to some tools and attitudes that you will need before you start on this journey. Your real 'why', the idea that drives your life's goals and ambitions, will be explored. The 'why' is the key to ensuring that the drive, energy, passion, and motivation required to reach the level of success you desire is maintained.

We will also introduce the concept of the vision board, how it can help map out what your success means to you, and also keep you anchored during those times of distraction or hardship, which you will inevitably encounter during your journey.

Your chances of achieving success are much greater if you understand why you are doing what you are doing and use it to support and accelerate your actions towards your vision.

Your vision is how you see your life in the future - where you want to be, categorised into a variety of areas described later in this chapter (such as family success, financial success etc).

Your vision of success and plan to achieve it breaks down into three levels:

- **WHY** – Your vision – What do you want your life to look like, what do you want to achieve?
- **HOW** – Your vehicle to achievement – How will you achieve your vision? Will it be through a job, a business, or a not-for-profit organisation? Will it be on your own, in a partnership, or in a team?
- **WHAT** – Your action steps – Where are you now and what exactly do you need to do next to make progress towards achieving your vision and why?

You need to work out what you want, what your ultimate goal is and reverse engineer it from there. Reverse engineering means knowing where you want to be or what you want to achieve and working backwards from that. If you do not start with the end in mind, you will only achieve your goals by pure luck, or more likely, not at all.

By the end of this chapter you will understand the difference between these levels, how they are connected, and you will have documented your 'why' (vision), your 'how' (vehicle) and 'what' (actions steps).

You Define Success

You woke up this morning – therefore, you are a success!

But, before you put this book down thinking that is all you need to know, there is a whole world out there to explore and one that you can make a positive impact on.

Success is defined as the accomplishment of a positive objective. A person might define success as having achieved a goal, big or small, in their lives. A business might define success as hitting targets set within the organisation, or an acquisition gone to plan. Success can also be the overcoming of a negative event in your life. There is an infinite number of definitions of personal and business success.

Success is a journey and not a destination. However, we can measure progress along the way and this is a common theme throughout this book: measurement of your progress. Measuring your progress will mean that you will be more likely to achieve your goals, no matter how big they are.

One thing you need to know from the get-go is that the path to success is seldom a straight line. You will have great days where you feel like nothing can stop you, and you will experience down days where you question everything. This is perfectly natural.

Below are the top three definitions of success given by the people we have interviewed in Your Success Podcast. Surprisingly, what you may expect to be at the top, money, is in fact in third place.

The top three definitions of what success is as defined by Your Success Podcast interviewees are:

1. Freedom to do what you want, when you want.
2. Ability to spend more time with family.
3. Money.

Let's expand on each of these and delve deeper into what exactly was said about them.

1. Freedom to do what you want, when you want.

The best definition we have of freedom is freedom of choice: the choice to spend your time with who you want, when you want. In the work environment this could be working only on projects you love, surrounded by great people who motivate you rather than drag you down, or not having to join your work colleagues for that dreary Christmas dinner that you feel you have to attend. Or, it could simply be the time freedom to paddle board with your dog on the sea, with not a care in the world. No targets or deadlines – just the freedom to enjoy yourself.

2. Ability to spend more time with family.

A recurring theme that has arisen in the podcast is regret: regretting not being able to spend more time with family, especially with children as they are growing up. Allowing or being driven by work commitments and not prioritising the family high enough. The ironic thing is that you can spend lots of time with your family when you have retired but by then the children have grown up and you will have missed their formative years.

3. Money.

Money wasn't number one, but it is in the top three. The need for money as a unit of exchange is prevalent in our society. Money is both of practical use such as buying food or a home, but it is also used as a measurement of success by some individuals when comparing themselves to other people, or as an individual measure of one's own success.

Although not top, money is certainly a factor related to the top two choices "freedom" and "spending more time with family". Money can be seen as a facilitator, affording you more freedom and flexibility.

We often hear that money is the root of all evil. However, money is neither good nor bad, it is simply a tool that can be used to exchange one thing for another. It is up to the individual how they spend their money, whether for good or ill.

How Do You Define Your Success?

As mentioned in the introduction, much of what people define as their success is actually based on what other people (the media, friends, family, colleagues) believe to be success.

It is hard not to be 'programmed' in this way in today's media led society: where everything is instantly on show for the world to see and where people are influenced by images of how they should look or behave. A perfectly filtered, wrinkle-free utopian image can easily be portrayed for the world to see – but is that always the reality?

If today you say you are a success, then who is going to argue otherwise? Of course, there are many different levels of success and many metrics you can set for yourself to gauge success. These can both be subjective and objective.

An astronaut might not consider themself a success unless they land on the moon. Yet, they possess piloting and scientific qualifications that an Air Force pilot or science undergraduate would rate highly in their measure of success.

A Formula 1 driver has incredible driving skills and reflexes when on the track, but wouldn't consider himself a success unless he is standing on the number one spot on the podium. Yet, someone who has failed their driving test three times would say passing their driving test is a great success. The fact is, even the Formula 1 driver had to start by learning how to drive.

The point here is that we all have to start somewhere and grow throughout our lives. What we consider a success at age 10 is likely to be quite different a mere 10 years later when we are 20. Throw a partner and children into the mix and suddenly the definition of success will change again for that person.

Health issues can also dramatically alter what we consider to be a success in our lives. The simple act of staying alive can be considered a success in itself. As you approach the later years of your life, you will become more reflective; what mattered and what drove you aged 20 or 30 will matter less, and your definition of success might simply be seeing your grandchildren develop.

Success and Excellence

Excellence in any field is usually noticed and people or companies who achieve excellence are then regarded as leaders in their respective field and are, therefore, considered a success. They create a new standard, are looked at with admiration and are often emulated by their peers and descendants.

What could be considered excellence?

- Curing a disease;
- Creating a high-quality product;
- A solution to a problem that helps society;
- An outstanding achievement such as being the first person to set foot on another planet;
- Creating something that is above the standard of others, and in doing so, creating a new standard for others to aspire to.

How Can You Become Excellent?

Maybe your success plan isn't as big as landing on the moon – most people's isn't – but maybe you want to be the very best in what you do on a day-to-day basis. Perhaps it is being excellent at your job and going above and beyond what your colleagues do, so that you stand out and can take personal pride in your achievement.

Becoming excellent takes time unless you are lucky enough to be born with a gift, such as being a musical genius like Mozart. Otherwise, it will take consistent action over a long period of time and continuous self-improvement to hit the heights of excellence. This is explored in more detail in Chapter 9 - Action!

Materialism and Success

Sometimes people turn to materialism to prove to themselves (and more often than not, to prove to others) how successful they are, by buying and displaying expensive items or trinkets to attract admiration and respect. The point is that you can be a success with or without money.

Let us compare and contrast these two successful, yet very different people, who have changed the course of history with their different ways of thinking and challenging the status quo, and who used possessions (or lack thereof) to prove their points.

Diogenes vs Howard Hughes

vs

The Curious Case of Diogenes

Let us introduce you to a peculiar individual who has been admired and researched for over 2,000 years. He gave us a new style of philosophy, and therefore is a success in his own right, but he is also the antithesis of materialism.

Diogenes was born in Greece in around 412BC. You could call him a very disruptive individual: frequently interrupting and behaving contrary to social norms, rejecting the cultural conventions of the time. He saw a society whose values were both corrupt and confused. Diogenes made living in poverty a virtue, choosing to beg for a living. He even slept in a large ceramic pot in the market!

Diogenes was one of the founders of Cynicism, which rejects conventional desires in favour of a moderate, simple lifestyle, but he took it to a whole new level. He chose to live as a homeless person, wandering naked around the market in Athens.

He prided himself on not having the possessions that most people at the time would consider essential. He did, however, have a little wooden cup for drinking water. Then one day, he happened across a boy drinking water using just his hands and he threw the cup down and exclaimed, "Fool that I am, to have been carrying superfluous baggage all this time!"

Another example of his unique way of thinking is what he said to none other than Alexander the Great. One sunny day, Diogenes was sitting in the street when the mighty Alexander the Great arrived and stood in front of him. Remember that Alexander the Great was a very powerful king, having conquered the lands from Greece to India and effectively had most of the known world's wealth available to him. Alexander said to Diogenes, "If I could offer you anything in the world, what would it be?" And what was Diogenes' reply? "For you to get out of my sunlight".

This is the equivalent of Queen Elizabeth II standing in front of a homeless person in the middle of the street, offering anything the homeless person desired, and the homeless person simply replying by asking her to stop blocking the sun! You have to admire Diogenes for his virtues!

Out of his absolute rejection of materialism, he helped inspire a school of Cynic philosophy alongside others. Cynicism in Ancient Greece meant living your life with virtue and living alongside nature, rejecting conventional desires such as wealth, power, sex and so on. Essentially, it was about leading a simple life.

Now let's contrast Diogenes' extreme example to another.

The High-Flying Howard Hughes

Howard Hughes was an extremely talented man, born in 1905. He was a pilot, an ultra-successful businessman, a film director, and philanthropist. He was also one of the wealthiest men in the world! He owned lots of land and real estate in and around Las Vegas. He developed his own planes to set world records with, bought radio stations and created movies; suffice to say he was extremely wealthy and he made sure the world knew it!

Hughes was a prolific real estate investor, often buying up large swathes of undeveloped land in and around Las Vegas. This then extended to owning hotels, more real estate, and media outlets – including some radio stations. He was responsible for changing the image of Las Vegas, which up until then had been seen as a Wild West kind of place, to how it is perceived today. He encouraged investment into the city and is responsible for making the city what it is today. Not content with this, Hughes was an avid flyer. To scratch this itch, he formed the Hughes Aircraft Company where he went on to set many world records and created many custom aircraft.

Hughes wanted to understand "the genesis of life itself" and therefore founded the "Howard Hughes Medical Institute": a not-for-profit medical research organisation in the United States of America. It was founded in 1953 and is still one of the largest funding organisations for medical research in the world, investing approximately $825 million per year into biomedical research.

Which of these two individuals would you consider to be the more successful? Who has left the bigger or better legacy? The man who had no worldly possessions except his intellect and philosophy, and whose ideas still influence philosophy to this day thousands of years on? Or the extraordinary businessman who created an amazing medical research investment company that continues to help medical research long after his passing, and will continue to do so for many years to come?

It could be argued that both are equally successful, and the point here is that you don't necessarily need to have great wealth or poverty to make a difference and be successful – the difference is made by the person who wants to make an impact on society.

Materialism is neither good nor bad, but it is good to have perspective with this. You will deserve rewards, but keep it aligned with your vision and values as opposed to simply buying something because you are expected to keep up with the latest fashion – "keeping up with the Joneses". Defining your vision and values is explored in more detail in the next section.

Why – Your Vision

What do you want your life to look like? What do you want to achieve?

To define your vision, think about what you want your life to be like in a few years' time. It is important to think about your vision in terms of the categories listed later in this section of the book. See the action steps at the end of this chapter for exercises on creating your vision board.

You decide the time horizon for your vision: 1 year, 5 years, 10 years, 20 years, and remember to be ambitious but realistic. If you want to be an airline pilot, this won't happen in a week! See Chapter 4 - Determination and Perseverance, for more on patience.

Your Vision Board

As ultra-successful businessman and philanthropist Bill Gates famously said, "we always overestimate the change that will occur in the next two years and underestimate the change that will occur in the next ten. Don't let yourself be lulled into inaction."

Your vision board is simply a visual representation of what you want in your life and what you view as your success. This can be a piece of paper that you have hanging on the wall, it can be a document on the computer, or it can be magazine cut outs or hand illustrated drawings. The point is that it needs to be visual and visible! Don't include too much text as inspirational images work better. Make sure your vision board is visible as much as possible throughout the day - either on the wall at work or at home, as a screensaver on your phone/tablet, or on your computer.

You might have a picture of your dream job (astronaut, postman or musician), your dream car, your dream holiday, family goals, and so on. It is completely yours to add whatever you like – after all, it's your life you are designing!

What Are Your Drivers to Success?

To understand your drivers to success, or to put it another way, what really makes you tick, it is vital to not only understand yourself, but also what will sustain and motivate you in the long run when you are striving towards your success. Below are some questions to help prompt you to start thinking about what really motivates and drives you forward.

- Do you want to enjoy the finer things in life?
- Is it money and power that drive you?
- Would you like to make your parents proud of you?
- Do you have something to prove to someone – or even to yourself?
- Is your driver an ego-based driver? Do you want to be the very best at what you do, i.e. you want to show the world your talent?
- Do you want to make a real difference in the world?

Or, is it a combination of all these drivers?

Your vision board will be a guiding light for you and, as well as keeping you motivated when you are having good days, it will also help to remind you of why you are doing what you are doing. This is especially important when you face challenges or obstacles.

You decide on what your future looks like and it starts today with the simple act of creating a vision board.

To ensure that your vision board is well rounded, you should include the following categories:

Friends – do you make enough time for your friends, support them, and create memories together?

Family – do you make time for your family, supporting them, and appreciating them? If you have children, do you make time for them?

Health – do you look after your health? Do you eat well, exercise, and drink enough water? Do you drink a lot of alcohol or consume a lot of caffeine? Do you get enough sleep?

Career – is your career where you want it to be? If not, is it on the right track or do you need evaluate whether staying in your current position is really the best thing for you?

Love – do you give and receive love – not just with your partner, friends and family, but with everyone you come into contact with?

Spirituality – this can mean whatever you want it to mean, but it is often used in terms of morality, inner peace, connection with a higher being (if you are religious) or can simply mean 'mindfulness' and self-awareness. How do you rate your own spirituality?

Money – are your finances where you want them to be, or at least on the right track?

Fun – do you make time to have fun and enjoy life, or are you always working? Would your friends and family say you radiate energy when you walk into a room, or sap energy?

Your vision can, and will, change over time, and that is to be expected. This is because your vision is driven by your values (what you regard as a priority and what is important) and voids (what you regard as 'missing'); it is natural for this to change over time.

Someone starting their first job is likely to have a completely different 'why' compared to someone with a new born baby. Priorities change. What you love to do changes over time, especially if the novelty of certain things wears off.

For the founder of a not-for-profit organisation, their vision may be driven by a positive or negative experience they have had in their life. They may have seen someone do great charity work before and been inspired. Or they may have been so appalled by something they saw that they felt compelled to act.

Your vision will keep you motivated and inspired on your down days: days when not everything is going the right way. Having a 'higher purpose' for what you are doing means it is much easier to maintain motivation. You need to focus on your 'why', otherwise excuses and procrastination can take over.

Financial trinkets and material items are weak motivators for long term success, even if they provide short term happiness. While material items can be good and offer a level of happiness (and there is nothing wrong with that), they act simply as milestone flags for how far you have come in life. Most people rate experiences, time with friends and family, and freedom of choice as higher measures of success than material items. Material items certainly make life easier, and in some cases more enjoyable, but they are not the reason in and of themselves.

Another good reason for clearly defining your vision is that if at any point you are struggling with an action step, you don't just give up: you look to your 'why' and your vision and you will be encouraged to continue pressing on. The success trait of determination and perseverance is explored in more detail in Chapter 4.

By seeing your vision clearly articulated in front of you every day – perhaps even carrying it around with you – your brain will start to see a new future, as opposed to some concept that might happen. You have made it a reality in visual form and that will help you accept that perhaps, just perhaps, this might actually become a reality, which is a million miles further than just a concept in your mind that in all likelihood, will remain there.

As personal development expert and successful business owner James Marks stated on Your Success Podcast, episode 30, "once you take pen to paper and you write your vision and goals down, it makes it more personal. It makes a better connection".

It is well documented that writing down goals and making plans to achieve them greatly increases the likelihood of the goals being achieved compared to either storing the goals in your head or not having goals at all.

Once you have defined your vision, you can move on to the 'how': the vehicle to your success.

How – Your Vehicle to Success

The 'how' is the vehicle you are going to use to make your vision board a reality.

There are many different ways to get to the same outcome, but there are only a few paths that will leave you feeling truly inspired and motivated.

Ikigai is a Japanese concept that means 'reason for being', and this is how you can find a vehicle (your job, career, business, and so on) that will drive you towards your vision. When you find your reason for being, you have more fun, earn more money, make more of an impact and the work doesn't even feel like work!

Ikigai is the intersection of the following:

- What you love;
- What you are good at;
- What you can be paid for;
- What the world needs.

As you can see in the diagram:

- What you love and what you are good at is your 'passion';
- What you are good at and what you can be paid for is your 'profession';

- What the world needs and what you can be paid for is your 'vocation';
- What you love and what the world needs is your 'mission'.

Finding something that meets all of these is where you find your 'how' to achieve your 'why', or your vision.

Don't worry too much here if you aren't entirely sure how you are going to get to where you want to be. Like walking through fog and only being able to see a few steps ahead, all you can do is start to take steps in the right direction and watch as the path beyond becomes clearer. Provided you are meeting the requirements of the Ikigai diagram, a path will become evident as you progress. See the task at the end of the chapter to define your 'how'.

The next step is to move on to the 'what' – the immediate action steps that will drive you towards your vision.

What – Your Action Steps

Once you have your vision set, and you know what your vehicle is, you need to take action. This is the 'what'.

Here, we are not talking about half-hearted steps: we are talking about massive action, day in, day out. This is what separates successful people from the unsuccessful.

Often, the difference between winners and also-rans is down to the amount of action they have taken, more than having a superior product, service, or marketing strategy. This is covered in more detail in Chapter 9 – Action.

As property investor, Nicole Bremner, highlighted in Your Success Podcast episode 33, "Be prolific, not perfect. Just get out there and do it. Don't worry that it's not perfectly polished."

The 'what' consists of tangible goals (which are milestone check points), broken down into action steps.

For goals, remember they need to be SMART!

SMART stands for **Specific**, **Measurable**, **Achievable**, **Relevant** and **Time-bound.**

Specific – This means that a goal is detailed and not too high-level or generic. For example, 'go on holiday' is not specific, but 'go on holiday to Thailand in September for one week with my partner' is specific.

Measurable – There needs to be an objective way to measure the goal – either with numbers or timelines. For example, weigh 80kg by 1st June rather than 'lose weight'.

Achievable - Based on existing track records, is it achievable? For example, you can't train to be a doctor in a week!

Relevant - The goal needs to be in-line with your broader objectives or vision. How does achieving this goal support or progress other areas of your life? For example, someone who wants to become a personal trainer could start by helping out in a gym part time; this could be a great stepping stone towards the main goal. In contrast, working in a bar is not as relevant to this goal.

Time-bound - The goal must be measurable over a period of time, otherwise it will drift and not be achieved. Parkinson's Law states that 'work expands so as to fill the time available for its completion.' Therefore, goals must have a deadline.

If you find that you are procrastinating over a task, it may be because it is too big and needs breaking down into smaller tasks, as you are being overwhelmed by the enormity of the task. See Chapter 9 – Action for an example of how to break a big overwhelming task into smaller and more manageable chunks.

Where Are You Now and What Resources Do You Have?

A key element of working out the action steps required for you to get from where you are now to where you want to be, is an honest assessment of your current situation. This includes an assessment of what resources you currently have available (think time, money, expertise etc), as well as who you have in your network who can help you achieve your goals.

A tool that will help you understand your current situation and put your goals and aspirations into context is known as Maslow's Hierarchy of Needs. Abraham Maslow created an easy to understand theory about what motivates a human being. He identified a hierarchy of human needs and concluded that what most motivates us is seeking the next level of need to the one we have currently attained. At the base of the pyramid you have the most basic of human needs: air, food, water, sleep, and shelter.

As these basic needs are fulfilled, we strive to meet the next level of needs: safety and security. Personal safety, your home, job security, and so on. Provided the first two levels have been met, you will then focus on achieving the next level of need: love and belonging. This is where friendship, family, and a sense of connection lie. The next level is esteem: being recognised, respected, and valued for who you are and what you have achieved. This is also where status sits.

Finally, at the top is self-actualisation. This is where you really feel connected with both yourself and the world – you want to become the very best that you can be. This is ultimately what we all strive for!

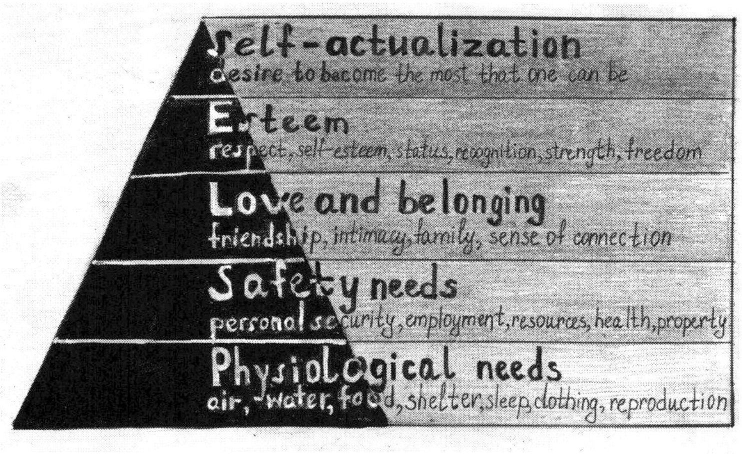

Notice that the first few levels are more concerned with physical needs, and as you ascend the pyramid, your needs reflect your inner state of being.

It is almost impossible for people to think about self-actualisation if they do not have shelter and food. This is true from both a psychological (they won't be able to handle that in their own minds) and physiological (they'll eventually die without food and shelter) point of view.

When defining your vision, why not aim big? Why not be the very best in your area/field? Why not aim to be the best actor, the best teacher, or the best scientist? Why not make a difference to this world?

You have a duty to leave this world a better place than it was when you entered it; leave a legacy that others can also aspire to and also inspire future generations.

Let's embark on this adventure to your success together!

Summary

- The definition of success is individual to you.
- Your 'why' is your vision, a clear articulation of what you want in life over a time period that you choose. Use a vision board to help document your vision and make sure it is placed somewhere that you will regularly see it.
- Your 'how' is your vehicle to success and is the intersection of the sections of the Ikigai diagram: what you are good at, what you love, what the world needs, and what you can be paid for.
- Your 'what' is the action steps that will take you from where you are now to where you want to be.
- Dare to think big!

Action Steps

1. Write down what success looks like to you. Be honest with yourself and filter out society's expectations of what success is.
2. Write down the names of five people you currently consider to be a success. Write down why you see them as successful.
3. Complete the Chapter 1 tasks in the Your Success Toolkit (available at www.yoursuccesspodcast.com/toolkit) including creating your Vision Board, finding your Ikigai, and defining your action steps to start working towards your vision.

NOTE: Do not be worried if you get stuck on any of these tasks. Further chapters will help you to formulate these ideas in greater detail and you can always come back and complete these action steps after you have finished reading the book.

Chapter 2

Motivation and Inspiration

SUCCESS TRAIT 2:
Successful people are inspired by their vision and can self-motivate

Motivation and inspiration are both very important traits that are required to be successful, but they are often confused with each other. This chapter will clearly lay out what each means, how you can access both and at what stages you need them to fulfil your potential and achieve your success.

By the end of this chapter, you will understand the differences between motivation and inspiration, be able to identify what your own motivators are, and discover what inspires you. You will also learn about the importance of accountability and how this can keep you on track. After all, the easiest person to deceive is yourself.

The concept of being in 'flow' will also be discussed in this chapter: how being in a state of flow will increase your productivity and ability to solve problems, as well as your enjoyment in getting things done.

Inspiration

Inspiration is defined as 'the process of being mentally stimulated to do or feel something, especially something creative'.

The simplest way to think of motivation and inspiration is that **inspiration** is a response to an external pressure or situation, whereas **motivation** comes from an internal desire to achieve something. That is why motivation can be great to get you started, but inspiration is the long-term fuel you need to keep going. Think of a flame that lights a fire as **inspiration** and the coal as the fuel that keeps you warm over a long period of time; that is **motivation**.

Motivators can be both positive and negative. A lazy employee will do just enough not to get fired, and that will be their motivation. Conversely, an inspired employee who enjoys their job and has their sights set on development and promotions within the company, will be inspired to put in the extra work required to do this of their own volition.

For self-employed people or business owners, the importance of being inspired to go to work (even if you are feeling demotivated and do not want to get out of bed) was highlighted by successful property investor and mentor Vicki Wusche in Your Success Podcast episode 40:

"It's not easy [being an entrepreneur]. You have to get yourself out of bed because no one else is going to tell you off if you show up to work late. No one's going to tell you off if you have a two-hour lunch break."

The greatest inspiration comes from knowing what your vision is (as described in Chapter 1) and aligning your goals and action steps to this, whilst doing work that you love to do, with people that you love to work with. It is this that will help get you through the challenges that you will no doubt face in your work and personal life.

Have you ever felt that sudden burst of creativity which then led to you coming up with a great idea or solving a big problem? This is a moment of inspiration and being in flow.

Think of motivation as a magnet that pulls you along your path to success whereas inspiration is the push that starts the journey in the first place. Inspiration will drive you to your destination and motivation is the fuel that powers you there.

What inspires you? Is it:

- A partner or loved one?
- Spending time with friends and family?
- Reading books or an inspirational speaker?
- Being part of a group and a sense of belonging?
- A positive or negative event in your life or within society?
- Doing something creative (listening to music, dancing, acting or art etc)?

Your inspiration could come from one or more of the above

and everyone's source of inspiration will be unique; you need to work out what truly inspires you.

Being in Flow

What Is Flow?

'Flow' or being 'in the zone' is a mental state where tasks become almost effortless, time flies by and you are completely focused and consumed by the activity. Being in flow can really accelerate your progress in anything you set your mind to. Imagine a motorway which is completely free of traffic, so you can put your foot down and drive with nothing to worry about apart from reaching your destination. That is what flow is: the uninterrupted state where you are operating at full speed to achieve your goals.

How to Get into Flow

People find their 'flow' in different ways, but things to think about are:

What you are doing – there will be certain tasks that you can get into flow doing – these may include cleaning, admin, discussing strategy, working on spreadsheets, it could be anything!

Who you are doing it with – there will be certain people who you work so well with that you are in flow when working on a project with them.

Why you are doing it – no doubt one of the most important pieces of the puzzle is why you are doing what you are doing. As discussed earlier in this chapter, you will get massive inspiration and internal energy from pursuing a path that leads to your vision.

Where you are doing it – controlling your environment is another key trait when achieving a state of flow. Do you work best in silence or do you need loud music playing for you to be in flow? Do you need an inspirational sea view, or do you work best in a dark room with no distractions? Controlling your environment is discussed in greater detail in Chapter 7.

Motivation

Motivation is defined as 'a reason for doing something'. Motivation comes from either moving towards pleasure or moving away from pain. Of the two, the strongest motivation comes from moving away from pain.

For example, being diagnosed with a serious health condition that is caused by 'lifestyle choices' like smoking, eating too much (bad) fat, salt, or sugar – is a much more powerful motivator to make changes in your life than the 'pleasure' of moving towards that dream body you have always desired.

As world memory champion and Guinness World Records holder David Thomas stated in Your Success Podcast episode 12:

“I’ve come to understand now, having been a professional speaker for 20 years, that nobody really moves unless there is a massive reward. Just an insane amount of reward, or huge pain. People don’t sit there and go, “You know what, I’m feeling a bit chubby. I’m going to go on a diet.” People wake up one morning, it takes them ten minutes to wash themselves, and they think, “Today’s the day”.”

You have to be committed to achieving an outcome, and this will come from either moving away from something that is painful in your life (being broke, being overweight, or being unemployed) or towards something that is positive (being financially stable, being healthy, or having a good job). Taking action is discussed in more detail in Chapter 9 – Action.

Often, this can mean re-framing what you want, into something that will have more of an impact on your own motivation. For example, it may not motivate you to think about the health benefits of eating well. Instead, it may be a stronger motivator to look at the detrimental effects that a bad diet is having on your body, to move you into action in this area of your life.

This also applies in a business environment, as business turnaround expert Peter Hill confirmed in Your Success Podcast episode 39:

"The businesses we have the most success with are those who feel they have no choice. They might be at risk of failure if they don't do something, so they just do exactly what we tell them. Businesses who are doing OK, who could do better, have to be persuaded quite carefully to play around with their prices, as they are worried about the impact of altering their pricing."

What motivates you? Is it:

- To be healthy?
- To be wealthy?
- To be recognised?
- To continuously learn?
- To prove someone wrong?
- To be the best at something?
- To be progressing forward in your life?
- To be successful (hence why you are reading this book)?

Only you know what truly motivates you, but it may take some time to discover what your motivators are, so be sure to make time to really delve into what pulls you forward.

Managing Energy Levels

Maintaining your energy levels and knowing how your energy levels fluctuate throughout the day is also key to your success and ensures maximum productivity

Some people work best in the morning, some during the day, and some late in the evening and into the early hours. There is no right or wrong time: the key is knowing your own best working times and building your working day around that.

Focus on the high value tasks that are most aligned to your vision and require the most attention at the times of the day that you feel you have the most energy.

High value tasks can be defined as what you are uniquely good at and add the most value. For most business owners, high value tasks are setting strategy, being a great leader, reviewing company financials and planning. Business owners should not be filling their time with low value operational tasks. If they spend all of their time on these, there will be no time left for the high value tasks as listed previously.

When a business is first created, the owner might do everything: defining strategy, dealing with the accounts, chasing sales, cleaning the office, and so on. However, as the business grows, the owner should be working on high level, income generating tasks and delegate low level business tasks to others.

Even within the high value tasks, there will be tasks that are more admin-heavy and require less deep-thought or creativity – these can be saved for the times of the day when you feel you have less energy or concentration. Alternatively, these tasks can simply be delegated to another person or outsourced completely as discussed in Chapter 7 – Environment.

Accountability

It is said, the easiest person to lie to, is yourself, which is why accountability is such an important part of success. Sometimes your motivation and inspiration levels will drop, and you will require a recharge and injection of new enthusiasm. We are much more consistent in our actions if we are accountable to someone else. This can be a partner or spouse, an employer, a teacher, a mentor, a friend, our business partner, or an employee. It can be anyone. The key is that our commitment to not let them down is stronger than our resolve to not let ourselves down.

This is why having a Personal Trainer who says they will meet you at the gym at 6am, massively increases the chances of you turning up at the gym at 6am, instead of just hitting that snooze button a few more times.

You can join accountability groups online or in person who meet regularly, or an online forum where members post their short-term goals and aspirations. Then, the other members of the group or an accountability partner will hold you to account so you don't slip or get side-tracked. There are many distractions in life which can take you off course, and there are many excuses you can tell yourself as to why you have not achieved the goals you set. The objective of an accountability partner or group is to hold you to account and not accept any of your excuses, in order to help you progress towards your goals.

Some examples of accountability groups (which are often coupled with some form of training, education or mentorship) are weight loss groups, business growth groups, personal training and fitness groups. There are accountability groups online for anything people are striving for and need support with.

Motivational accountability (such as having a personal trainer) is used regularly by those wanting to make a change in their life.

However, drawing inspiration from aligning your actions to your values is a longer term, more sustainable trait, which will really drive your success.

Summary

- You need both motivation and inspiration in your life, on your journey towards success, but finding something that inspires you into action is much better than responding to external motivators to get things done.
- The easiest person to lie to is yourself, which is why being accountable to other people can accelerate your path to success. You are in flow when tasks feel effortless and time flies. You are unstoppable, with laser-like focus, and the quality of your work increases dramatically.

Action Steps

1. What motivates you? Think about some motivators that get you motivated and write them down.
2. Think about something you are inspired to do, something that gives you energy, and no one has to ask you to do it; you just get it done. This could be art or another creative activity like taking the dog for a walk, business meetings, whatever! Write down five occasions when you have felt inspired and you have felt in 'flow' - when/where/what were you doing?
3. Complete the Chapter 2 tasks in the Your Success Toolkit (available at www.yoursuccesspodcast.com/toolkit) including writing down three people who you think could potentially be an accountability partner for you.

Chapter 3

Constant Learning and Growth

SUCCESS TRAIT 3:
Successful people are constantly learning and growing

Successful people never believe that they have all the answers or know everything there is to know. They value learning, they have a growth mindset, and believe in learning from everywhere and everyone.

As the philosopher Socrates once famously said, "I know one thing; that I know nothing."

Successful people also understand the value in learning from failure, and (provided that learnings are implemented in the form of personal, business, or process improvement) they know that failure actually helps them to grow.

This chapter will explore the success trait of constantly learning and growing, which is important because to be truly successful, there will be failures along the way and rather than trying to avoid failure at all costs, having an ability to embrace failure and learn from it is a key success trait.

Wisdom and knowledge can come from a variety of sources. You can learn from books, videos, and podcasts. You can learn by the act of performing a task, or shadowing somebody else and learning from them. You can learn through feedback and asking other people or customers to help you improve, and you can learn from people and companies in different industries and geographies.

The Value of Learning

In a constantly changing world, where people's expectations, business, politics, technology, and the environment are changing, we cannot simply stand still and expect to succeed. Everything is in a constant state of either growth or decay: if you don't maintain your car it will eventually stop working, if you stop maintaining your house it will decay and eventually collapse, if you stop running or lifting weights, your strength and stamina will decrease.

Therefore, if you do not invest (both time and money) in yourself and into your own learning, you will seriously jeopardise your chances of success – or at least slow down your progress.

Why not enhance and accelerate your success journey by standing on the shoulders of other experts to give yourself a head start?

Investing in your education is probably the second most important investment you can ever make, after your health.

Successful people place real value on education, and as such invest time and money into improving their mindset, skillset, systems, processes and relationships. Studies have shown that learning more can be directly linked to increased earnings, so it pays to learn!

All forms of education distil the collective wisdom from other people into organised, logical, manageable parcels of information that the 'student' can use to improve themselves. In today's world, it is not a lack of information that is the issue. The internet contains more information than could be consumed by anyone. The key is that the information needs to be collated in a way which can be usefully leveraged by anyone who wants to learn.

According to business magazine Inc.com, top CEOs and executives read four to five books per month. These are the people running the biggest companies in the world, responsible for hundreds of thousands of staff, and who have risen up the corporate ranks to become CEO. They still make the time and understand the value of reading four to five books per month. It is more than likely that, because they read those books and continue to educate themselves with new ideas, they have been able to scale the corporate ladder compared to someone who does not read regularly.

Now, becoming a top CEO may not be what you want in life, but the principle here is that you too can leverage the wisdom of others which has been distilled into, for example, a book, to improve your own chances of success and this applies not only to books but to all methods of learning.

For more information on moving from self-taught learning to training and mentorship and taking you to the next level, see Chapter 7 - Environment.

Growth Mindset vs Fixed Mindset

'Growth mindset' is a learning theory developed by Dr Carol Dweck, a Stanford University psychologist, who proposes that people who are open to the potential, can improve their own performance, ability, and intelligence. 'Fixed mindset' is the opposite, and refers to a belief that a person's talents are fixed and cannot be improved.

Remember, if you believe you can or you believe you can't, you are right!

Having either a growth or a fixed mindset when approaching anything in life will dictate how the person approaches a task, and also how they deal with any challenges or obstacles that they face.

The advantages of a growth mindset are:

- Reduced stress and emotional impact of failure.
- A desire to seek out feedback in order to improve.
- Resilience when faced with adversity / challenges.
- A level of comfort with approaching new tasks or situations.

To develop a growth mindset:

- Set high standards for what you want to achieve and stretch yourself. As humans, we are poor at predicting our own performance and can often surpass our own expectations when pushed. For example, when working with a personal trainer in the gym, we can often work harder than we thought possible. Likewise, when working with a mentor who supports you in solving a problem, you might find that you succeed when you believed that you would fail.

- Be persistent. Don't give up after one or two tries of something new and if something isn't working, put time and thought into problem solving rather than the easy option of giving up.
- Ask for feedback on the things you do at home, at work, or in your business.
- Remember to be open to feedback, whether constructive or negative and not to become defensive as this will close your mind to what could be valuable feedback, even if it is not what you would like to hear.

Learning from Everywhere

Learning can come from anywhere and everywhere, from anyone and at any time.

Companies can learn from businesses in other industries in order to improve. Just because they are not operating in the same industry, does not mean that there is no learning to be had!

Learning can also come from anyone. You do not just need to learn from people 'further ahead' of you in the journey. Yes, they will have valuable insights and this is why mentoring is mentioned in Chapter 7 – Environment, but there can also be learnings from peers and those who are 'behind' you in the journey. As you grow and develop yourself, your business, your systems, or your relationships, layers of complexity can often be added where they are not needed. Speaking to someone who is more 'green' or naïve may offer a fresh perspective on things and help you get to the root of an issue.

As a company in the customer services sector expands, it can often lose sight of the reason why the company was formed: to solve a problem for the customer. As such, a re-focus back to the core purpose of the company can be extremely valuable.

The key here is that learning can come from anywhere. So, be open to learning from anyone, anywhere and at any time.

Learning from Failure

There has no doubt been an experience in your life where you are glad that you have the knowledge gained from it, but you sure wish that you could have known it beforehand rather than learning the lesson the hard way.

As comedian Steven Wright once said, "Experience is something you don't get until just after you need it."

For example, you may need a certain level of experience to get a job, but you would have to have been working in the job to get the experience for the job you are applying for!

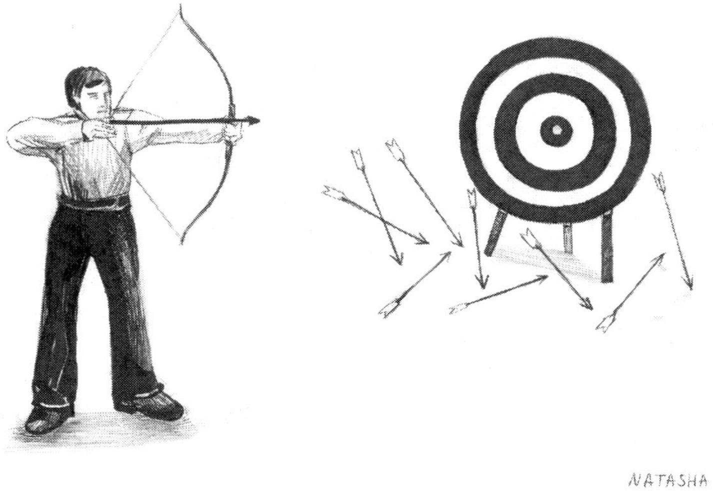

There are few easy ways of gaining experience without having gone through the learning phase, and usually it is via hardship or lessons learned.

Matthew Syed, in his book *Black Box Thinking*, contrasts the approach to learning from failure in the airline industry vs the healthcare profession.

In the airline industry, accidents and near-miss information is shared between plane manufacturers and plane operators to ensure that the learnings from them are fed back into process improvements and changes to manufacturing. This constant sharing of information and feedback loop means that the airline industry boasts an impressive safety record that is constantly improving over time. This is despite the fact that, on paper, flying at hundreds of miles per hour in a metal tin could be seen as one of the most dangerous ways to travel.

Contrast this with the medical profession, where there are frequent cover-ups, where incident reporting and process improvement information is not as widely and regularly shared, and where the culture does not embrace failure as openly, due to fear of exposure, a fear of being sued or damage to personal pride.

A single failure usually has a complex set of circumstances around it. What might, on the surface, appear to be a failure in a specific area, may actually be made up of failures in several areas that have all contributed towards the main, single failure. On this basis, it is important not to have a blame culture, as 'blame' rarely sits solely on one person or company.

It is also important to ensure that the same kind of failure does not happen again, you have to understand the full root cause of an issue to be able to implement changes at the root cause level, rather than at the final point of failure. Think of this like medicating for the symptoms of a condition, rather than addressing the underlying condition. This is similar to applying after-sun lotion on the sun burn after the fact, instead of looking at why you got burnt in the first place.

In addition to the benefits listed in the chapter so far, there are also significant physiological and psychological benefits to learning. For instance, reading is very stimulating for your brain and could help stave off dementia as well as the additional benefit of making you feel happier. Research has also shown that reading is relaxing and can help you sleep better which in this hyper-connected, always-on society, is a very good thing indeed.

Learning should be a lifelong mission as you should always be hungry to learn and grow. Ask yourself, apart from the information you can apply for your own uses, what could you pass on and help to inspire future generations?

Summary

- Successful people appreciate the value of education as a way to leverage the knowledge from those who have already done what they are trying to achieve.
- Successful people have a growth mindset (as opposed to a fixed mindset) and never believe that they know it all.
- Successful people know they can learn from anyone and anything – this can be people or companies in other industries or geographies and can be those more junior/less experienced as well as more senior/more experienced.
- Successful people learn from failure in order to improve (and this can relate to improving their mindset, skillset, systems, processes, relationships).

Action Steps

1. Think about your vision and your goals. What resources could you leverage to help you improve? Are there any books, podcasts, videos, training courses, or mentorship programmes that you could use to accelerate your path to success? Write these down.
2. Think about whether you have a fixed mindset or a growth mindset. If you have a fixed mindset in certain situations, think about the possibilities that could be open to you if you shifted to more of a growth mindset.
3. Complete the Chapter 3 tasks in the Your Success Toolkit (available at www.yoursuccesspodcast.com/toolkit) including creating a 'black box thinking' culture in your home and work environment.

Chapter 4

Determination and Perseverance

SUCCESS TRAIT 4:
Successful people are determined, and they persevere through challenges

Your vision is big and very important to you; you want to succeed and make your vision a reality.

You know that you need to make a big commitment to yourself to make your vision happen. Commitment is only half the battle though; you will need bucket-loads of determination and perseverance. How much you will need is difficult to assess, but at least you can prepare yourself for whatever situation might arise.

Sometimes, it isn't always the larger problems that knock you off balance – it can be the smallest of challenges that can create the most stress in your day.

You will also need to control and balance your emotions so that you are not constantly reacting strongly to negative events, or overreacting to positive events which leave you feeling crushed once the euphoria has died down.

Having a more even-keel approach will both help your decision-making process and happiness. Once this skill has been developed properly, you can adapt it to every aspect of your life.

Gratitude, perspective, and patience are key skills within the success trait of determination and perseverance – these are also covered in this chapter.

How Badly Do You Want Success?

Sometimes success can be the mother of necessity and will come to those who have no other choice but to succeed. Two noteworthy examples of this are Alexander the Great and Abraham Lincoln.

No Plan B for Alexander the Great

When Alexander the Great started his campaign to conquer Persia in 334BC, he was massively outnumbered and his supplies were nowhere near as plentiful as those of the country he was invading. His army was fearful and hesitant once they realised just how outnumbered they really were. Therefore, he had to give his troops a clear and hard-hitting message of confidence and fearlessness. He ordered all the boats to be burned. There was to be no plan B! Alexander and his troops were to make this a success, or they would die trying.

This kind of message, where there is no other option but to succeed, with major consequences if you don't, really sharpens a person's resolve to do well.

Alexander and his army went on to conquer from Greece to India, and understood the importance of integrating different cultures by marrying soldiers in his army to local people. His battle tactics are still taught today at military schools in the UK and America. He also facilitated the spread of Hellenism across the Middle-East and beyond, which is still felt to this day. Not bad for someone who died aged just 32! What a legacy!

Abraham Lincoln, The Man Who Would Not Give Up

Here is a man who just would not give up.

Abraham Lincoln is known as the man who led America away from the blight of slavery, even if he had to fight a civil war across a divided nation. He was also a businessman and an inventor and remains the only President to ever register a patent – his invention was a device to lift boats over shallow ridges or rocks in a river!

Lincoln was born in 1809 in Kentucky, United States, into humble surroundings. By the end of his life, he had risen to the highest office of the land, The President of the United States of America – a remarkable achievement! During his life, Lincoln suffered many setbacks and tragedies, but this did not stop him from moving forward.

Lincoln started a store with a business partner which then failed and left them both in debt. To make matters worse, his business partner died, meaning that even more debt passed over to Lincoln. He suffered from depression after breaking off his engagement and two of his four children died during his lifetime. He also lost elections on his way to becoming President.

Any single one of these events would be enough to stop the average person, but Lincoln was different. He had the traits of determination and perseverance by the bucket-load and look at how much he achieved despite his many setbacks.

No matter what life threw at him, Lincoln would not stop. This is how you need to be to achieve your vision of success. If it is that important to you then you must not stop, no matter what life throws at you.

Overcoming Adversity

Adversity. When things go wrong. Roadblocks.

On your success journey, it is simply a case of *when* you will encounter these, rather than *if*. Just as certain as the Earth orbits the Sun, you will encounter problems along your success journey. A part of success trait four is that successful people persevere through challenges and overcome adversity when it strikes. If you are doing anything meaningful or pushing yourself to achieve greatness, adversity will hit you in one form or another and it will be your resolve to overcome these challenges that sets you apart from others.

A truly inspirational story of perseverance is that of Mark Ormrod.

Ormrod was a Royal Marine serving in Afghanistan. On Christmas Eve 2007, he was out on a routine foot patrol when he stood on and triggered an IED (Improvised Explosive Device), which meant that he had to have both his legs amputated above the knee and his right arm amputated below the elbow. He was the UK's first triple amputee to survive the Afghanistan conflict. He was told he would never walk again, but Mark is not someone to just admit defeat. At this point, he could have quite easily accepted this fact and resigned himself to using a wheelchair for the rest of his life.

Instead, Mark grew even more determined to prove the doctors wrong. Slowly but surely, he began the long and painful journey back to a position where he can now not only walk, but has competed in the Invictus Games, fundraised for military charities, and inspired people all over the world to not only accept their situation, but strive to be the best they can be. Here's an excerpt from the interview with Mark Ormrod in Your Success Podcast episode 36:

"We're surrounded by so much negativity in life. A few years ago, I changed my whole morning routine. I used to get up in the morning, put the news on and listen to all of the negative things that were going on in the world, then I'd have a shower, throw some breakfast down my neck, get in my car and listen to more negative news on the radio. Then I'd usually get stuck in traffic or be cut up by someone on the road and get mad about it and by the time I got to work or wherever it was I was going I'd want to kill myself because it was so depressing. So I decided to change everything: what I did in the morning, what I did in the day, everything – because I knew that if I wanted to change my life and the way I felt, I needed to change my daily habits and routines.

So, I started reading books on self-development. I stopped watching & listening to the news and I started listening to podcasts and audiobooks instead. In life you'll come across people who will tell you, "You can't do this. You can't do that." In the beginning I got told, "You'll never be able to walk." and when I did the charity fundraising, "you can't bungee jump because it's not safe." And I was like, "well, I can, I just need to figure out a different way." and then I started doing it and realising that a lot of this stuff is just people's opinions, not facts, and I wasn't willing to let it stop me living life on my terms, the way I wanted to do it. And the more I got on with it, I thought, "Do you know what? I'm in charge of this. You can tell me your opinion, you can tell me what you think is going to happen, but ultimately, I'm the only one who can decide and make it happen."

As well as major, life changing single events, there are also smaller, more irritating events that happen to us that grind us down, constantly scratching at you; they drain both your time and emotional stability. It is important to address those issues as soon as possible before the small problems start building into something much bigger.

Attack of the Tiny Mosquitos

If you are bitten by a mosquito, you can usually handle it without too much drama. Sure, the aftermath is annoying for a few days, but you forget about it relatively quickly. However, if you get bitten by a few mosquitoes over a week, the effects start making their way into your conscious mind and your day can be one constant itch. Keep getting bitten by many mosquitoes over a few days and then you have a problem. Something needs to be done about it as it will grind you down and quite possibly affect your well-being and decision-making processes.

What is the relevance of mosquitoes to you? Working on your success plan and the problems that you will experience can sometimes feel like an attack of tiny mosquitoes: day in, day out, biting you and sometimes there is no end in sight. For example, you can handle one small problem – no problem at all. Two or three problems in a week? Bring it on. You can sort them out in no time. Having a few problems, whilst irritating, can be handled with relative ease but what if you have lots of little problems compounded over many weeks? It can grind you down, but you need to be ready for this.

You need to have the tools in place to handle or delegate the problems to others who either have the capacity to handle the problems, or are more qualified to sort out the problems for you.

This is just as relevant in your personal life as it is in your work life. Individual challenges in life can be dealt with relative ease. However, if a few challenges arise at around the same time, this can really grind you down. It is how you react to the situation and fix these problems when they arise that is important. Even small issues stacked up upon each other can lead to overwhelm and a crippling effect in your decision-making ability.

For example, you receive a phone call from your brother saying that he has broken his leg after falling off his quad bike and needs you to bring some things to the hospital. With great concern, you jump into your car, race to the hospital and you see two bright flashes; you have just been caught by a speed camera. You curse yourself. You arrive at the hospital and just as you are about to step inside, you receive a phone call from your boss and she wants to see you in the morning for a meeting. You ask what it is about, but she says it is best to talk in person. This leaves you feeling apprehensive.

You see your brother lying on the hospital bed and you are already feeling quite tense on top of the worry for him, and then he asks you to pick his quad bike up from where he crashed it and return it back to his garden.

The next day, you have the meeting with your boss and your gut feeling was correct, the company are making cutbacks and they have decided to let you go. This week is not going well, and it is only Tuesday!

You finish the day at work feeling down and annoyed. You receive the speeding fine letter and you just want to sit down and relax. Then you remember you have to take your brother's quad bike back to his garden, so you drive to the farm and load the bike onto the trailer. As you are reversing out of the farm, you scrape your car bumper on the side of a wall and you ask yourself, "why is this happening to me?"

Each one of these issues, whilst concerning or inconvenient, can be handled with relative ease. However, when they compound together, they can lead to a feeling of helplessness as you are overwhelmed.

Look at each problem in isolation and think about the solution, rather than as a load of issues grouped together. The key is that each of the issues can, individually, be handled with ease, so that is the way to approach dealing with them.

The other key trait here is taking ownership and responsibility for your life, which is covered in detail in Chapter 5.

Adaptability is also a key skill in overcoming adversity. The ability to change your approach in response to challenges that you face will mean you are more flexible in your approach. There are many ways to get to the same outcome. Just as there are many roads to one destination, your current path may be blocked. Despite this, you can take an alternative route which, although it may take longer, may be more scenic or may open up other opportunities along the way that you did not foresee. A diversion isn't always a bad thing.

It's Okay to Have Down Days, But...

This journey you are undertaking, this rabbit hole that you are going down, will throw many hurdles and obstacles at you and there will be some days where you will feel down, deflated, or discouraged, leaving you to question the very reason why you started this in the first place!

It is OK to feel this way, at least temporarily anyway. If you feel down constantly, then perhaps your vision needs to be revisited to see why you now loathe what you initially loved. Maybe you can meet your mentor or speak with your accountability partner and get a fresh perspective on why things aren't going the way you planned.

No matter who it is, and no matter how successful they are, everyone has experienced down days. The most important element of this is how you return to a normal state and how you pull yourself back out of the down state and get back to full power.

It could be that you are attempting to complete too many tasks that are not aligned to your values or vision or take you out of your flow. Re-focusing back on what you love to do can help you recover from down days and get you back on track. See Chapter 2 – Motivation and Inspiration for more on flow. Perhaps you are working very long hours, and this is affecting your physical and mental health, so a break could do you the world of good in the short term. The long term solution will be to analyse why you are having to work the long hours and put a system in place where you are offloading some of the lower value tasks to others who can support you. A rested you means a happier you, which in turn leads to making better decisions!

Do not let a down day or week jeopardise your success journey. If you get a flat tyre on your car, you don't go out and shoot the other three!

As Royal Marine, Mark Ormrod said in Your Success Podcast episode 36:

"I think it's very normal to have a down day. You can't fight it all the time and just keep resisting it. Sometimes, having an outburst or release is the healthiest thing to do and then you draw a line under it and say "Right, we're done now. I've finished feeling sorry for myself. Let's focus on what needs doing"."

Even a tough, elite Royal Marine says it's OK to have a down day once in a while; let it all out and move on.

Gratitude and Perspective

Having gratitude for the small things in life and making sure you retain perspective is essential for long-term success.

Gratitude is appreciating what you have, whilst perspective is understanding that even though what you have is not what you want to have in a month, a year, or a decade, it is still a lot more than some people have and more than you yourself had at an earlier stage in your journey.

The fact is, that in their very nature, aspirational people who are striving for success always look forward and at goals in the future. This works well as it focuses the mind on what needs to be done to achieve these goals, but you cannot live solely in this state; you will never be satisfied as there is always more to achieve.

There is a delicate and ever-changing balance between gratitude and aspiration. **They are almost polar opposites in that gratitude says, "be grateful for what you have" and aspiration says, "I'm not where I want to be."**

The fact is, success requires gratitude. Living in a solely aspirational state will leave you constantly frustrated by a lack of progress.

When things are not going your way and it seems days, weeks, or even months have been a struggle, perhaps it is time to get another perspective on things. Who can you talk to about things? By talking about your problems, you are allowing a fresh pair of eyes to look at your problems and maybe offer a solution that you hadn't considered.

I Want It All Now!

Patience, patience, patience!

We get it, you want to accelerate your success journey as fast as possible. However, if the goal is worth it, it will probably require a huge amount of effort and time.

Are you truly committed to completing this journey? We want you to feel inspired and have the tools that you need to make this journey amazing and achieve every success you put your mind to, but you will encounter struggle and toil through your journey.

As Personal Trainer James Jordan discussed in Your Success Podcast episode 23:

"It's all about consistency. People want results yesterday, they forget it's taken them three or four years to put that weight on, but they want it off in four weeks – that doesn't really measure up, does it?"

Rushing a worthy goal such as your success journey, could result in you burning out too early, or making poorly thought-out or hastily-planned decisions. It can also jeopardise your chances of achieving success. We have all heard of Aesop's fable of the Tortoise and the Hare, where it was the slow and steady tortoise that wins the race. This is how you should be. Moderate your impatience and temper your pace so that you can maintain your energy levels and enthusiasm over the long term.

Go Easy on Yourself

Rome wasn't built in a day, but look at how long it survived!

Remember to go easy on yourself during your success journey. Don't overreact or beat yourself up too hard if you do not meet the ambitious goals you have set for yourself.

For example, if you set a goal to get 20 clients in your first year of business, but you only secure 10, it can be demoralising.

Yes, the target has been missed in that it is not 20, but it is 10 more than you had at the beginning of the year. Putting things into perspective is so important to the success of your long-term plan.

Let's take a moment to think about Ancient Rome, an amazing empire that achieved so much and still impacts on us all to this day. It all started in a small village in central Italy, but at its peak the Roman Empire stretched from Scotland to Northern Africa, from Wales to Persia (modern day Iran), encompassing an estimated population of 57 million people!

How does a small village grow into such a goliath? Was it an overnight success or was there a phenomenal amount of effort made over centuries to achieve it all? Of course, we don't have centuries to spare but we can start today and get that idea, that business, that career you always wanted off to a good start. To quote our Ancient Roman friends, "Carpe diem" – Seize the day!

Although the Roman Empire no longer exists, it could be argued that the idea of Rome still survives today, within Christianity. Rome still has not left us quite yet.

The Creative Hurricane

The Creative Hurricane is a good way to think about your success journey. When working on a great endeavour you will come across lots of obstacles, which you will overcome. That has become your nature – you find solutions, not problems. You have been working for months, if not years, on your success plan and the results, after the number of hours and phenomenal hard work, should be slowly revealing themselves.

Perhaps the results aren't showing up as quickly as you had anticipated, or maybe it is a lot harder than you thought possible, or it's possible that you are spinning lots of plates simultaneously. This is when you need to stop, take a day or two off, and look back at where you have come from and appreciate the results that you have actually achieved so far.

Think of your journey like a (creative) hurricane. It passes through a region of land and where it passes it disturbs the status quo, similar to what you are doing with your life and the disruption your journey is causing around its surroundings. You are moving at a good speed and nothing is going to stop you, but inside every hurricane is an eye: the peaceful part of the hurricane. This is where you will pop your head up, look backwards, and reflect on what you have achieved and express gratitude for how far you have travelled. Yes, the road ahead is long and there will still be uncertainties, but you are so much closer to achieving your success compared to when you first started.

In the time you have been working hard on your success, what new skills have you learnt? What new contacts have you added to your network? How much money have you made? What doors have you knocked on? What opportunities have you discovered or created? Would you have done any of this had you not started on your journey?

This ties directly into gratitude and appreciation for both yourself and what you have and will achieve in the future.

Remember, more energy is spent when you first start your car to get it moving than travelling at top speed; it is that initial push that gets the momentum going.

Long-Term Thinking

When starting out on your journey, you usually start with great ambition in your first year. We fully support having big audacious goals for year one but just be conscious that if you don't achieve them, it could be quite demoralising. Conversely, when setting 10-year goals, people often don't set big enough goals as they underestimate what they can achieve. Let's run a little exercise. **Ask yourself the following:**

What have you achieved in the past 10 years?

A question to ask yourself and a good chance for some honest reflection is what have you learnt and what milestones have you achieved in the past decade. This will help you achieve perspective and gives you a comparison between what you have been doing in your current state versus what you could do with more focus and more time dedicated to achieving your success.

A decade is both a long time and a short time in terms of your success. You no doubt will have achieved lots of small successes, which are hopefully already compounding into something bigger. But sometimes your success journey will span multiple decades, as your vision is so vast, or it simply requires that amount of time to bring it to fruition.

The decisions you make today will affect where you will be in one year and beyond, so decide wisely. When starting your success journey, you will no doubt have to make lots of seemingly insignificant decisions day to day. **Do not lose sight of the bigger picture.**

Mastering Boredom

Boredom – the arch enemy of productivity and creativity. Do yourself a favour and remove this word from your vocabulary. Get rid of it right now. Good bye, boredom, good bye.

But why should you ban the word? The reason for doing this is because you are what you say. Research has shown that the language you use both internally (what you think) and externally (what you say out loud) can reflect and form your state of being, whether that is positive or negative. For more on this, see Chapter 8 – Communication.

We all have periods of inactivity where the newly-banned word can creep in but let us offer you a quick and easy way to cure and prevent it from easily returning.

To live a happy and contented life, you will need:

- A hobby to keep you creative;
- A hobby to make you money;
- A hobby to keep you fit.

Imagine if you could combine all three hobbies into one activity!

If you can find or create the above three hobbies and regularly enjoy doing them, then the banned word shouldn't resurface again, and you will create great positive habits which will keep you entertained, happy, and healthy way into the future.

The One-Degree Difference

Imagine you are hiking with some friends, using a map and compass (old school for sure, but your GPS has a flat battery) to navigate to your destination, a nice warm hotel 30 kilometres away. You begin navigating confidently but you soon realise after a few hours that you have made a mistake and have been walking ever so slightly away from the correct route, in your estimation by only a degree or so. What started out as a tiny, almost imperceptible difference in direction has now amplified into a large deviation from the proper route, and after a few hours, that has caused many extra kilometres to be added to your hike.

This is how it is in life: small changes in a positive direction can become good habits, which over time, will create big positive changes that are happening because of them.

Equally, the opposite is true. Small bad habits in your life can amplify into much bigger problems. Often you do not see the bad habits happening or growing, certainly not enough to do anything about them, but fast-forward many weeks and months and they start to become noticeable. Eventually, you will need to address them, probably with considerable effort to reverse the damage.

Keep an eye on the one-degree difference. This also known as compounding which is explained in more detail in Chapter 9 – Action.

This is why having your vision board close to hand is essential, so you remain on target and focused. For example, just because your computer isn't working properly today, doesn't mean your plans for the whole week will be derailed.

Stay focused. Your vision of success will keep you anchored!

Sacrifice for Success and Embrace Delayed Gratification

"Today I will do what others won't, so tomorrow I can accomplish what others can't."

-Jerry Rice

This is such a powerful statement. We all want to achieve great success, whatever our definition of that is, and have the freedom to do whatever we want, whenever we want as there is no greater gift in life than freedom. Why then, do so many people not achieve these goals?

Personal freedom, financial freedom, and time freedom – these are some of the most strived-for goals. But are you willing to put in the hard work, sacrifice, and patience required to achieve them?

Will you read a personal development book or work on progressing your success plan when your friends are enticing you out for a drink or other seemingly harmless distractions, similar to modern-day Sirens (Sirens were dangerous creatures in Greek mythology, they lured sailors towards rocks with their voices and enchanting music, eventually causing the sailors to be shipwrecked).

Will you invest some of your savings into the business you always wanted to start, or will you be tempted to buy the nice new car?

Will you give up buying daily coffees and other niceties in the short term, so you can save and buy your dream home?

Are you committed to achieving your success plan, or will you be distracted like a magpie when it sees a nice new shiny object?

There are trade-offs here for sure, but isn't achieving your success worth it? If not, then revisit your vision and your 'why', and set a stronger vision for yourself. Your 'why' needs to be rock-solid, aligned with your values and what you want from life.

Summary

- You will face adversity on your journey to success and it is your level of commitment and determination that will dictate your level of success.
- It's OK to have down days when you feel like everything is conspiring against you. It won't last forever, so just remind yourself of why you started in the first place and do not give up. Your vision board will help you here.
- Being grateful and having perspective on how far you have come and what you have achieved will help you when things get tough.
- You have to be patient. Anything worth having takes time, hard work, and determination. Rome wasn't built in a day but look how long it lasted.
- There will be sacrifices that you have to make for success, but these will be worth it if you are truly moving towards your vision.

Action Steps

1. Take stock of how far you have come and feel thankful for where you are, even if you do have many issues to contend with. What are you grateful for right now?
2. What brings your mood down regularly and what can you do about it? Who can encourage you on those down days?
3. Complete the Chapter 4 tasks in the Your Success Toolkit (available at www.yoursuccesspodcast.com/toolkit) including thinking about the past ten and next ten years.

Chapter 5

Ownership and Responsibility

SUCCESS TRAIT 5:
Successful people take ownership and responsibility for their life, and do not live with regret

This chapter explains the importance of taking ownership and responsibility for everything in your life as a way to ensure you retain control over your life, what happens within it, and plot your path to success.

The reason why excuses do not support you on your success journey is also detailed in this chapter. We have all given or heard excuses at some point in our lives. Too often, excuses are used as a justification for why a certain outcome has occurred and this can prevent progress towards the vision of your success.

Regret is also discussed in this chapter, both in terms of not regretting missing out on business or career opportunities and ensuring that whilst on your success journey, you do not neglect making memories outside of your success plan and spending quality time with friends and family.

Ownership and Accountability

The importance of ownership and accountability cannot be understated, but, what is meant by ownership and accountability?

Ownership is taking control of a situation and not just passively sitting by and watching it happen. If you can see that something is not going in the right direction, you step in and offer support, guidance, or leadership (if required) to get the activity or task back on track.

Accountability is taking responsibility for an outcome, after it has happened, to either yourself or someone else – whether it is good or bad. Too often, people are more than happy to take credit for something that has gone well and be the hero. Far fewer people are prepared to stand up and take responsibility for something that has not gone so well.

When ownership and accountability is discussed in this chapter, it refers to both the approach and attitude going in to a task as well as taking responsibility for the outcome, good or bad. The reason why ownership and accountability are such important success traits is because they allow you to take control of your life.

As author, speaker and life coach Hal Elrod is famously quoted as saying:

"The moment you take responsibility for everything in your life is the moment you can change anything in your life."

Most people think events happen to them and they have little or no control over them. However, in the majority of cases, there is either something that could have been done to avoid the situation happening, or a positive learning result that can occur from the situation (turning a negative experience into a positive). These two ideas are explored in more detail below.

Here are some examples of taking ownership to avoid negative outcomes:

- If you receive a speeding ticket, the best way to avoid it happening again is to leave earlier and not have a need to exceed the speed limit. Don't blame the Police for putting the speed camera there.
- If your wallet is stolen from the passenger seat of your car, the best way to prevent this happening again is to remove the temptation and take it out of the car when you park. Don't blame the opportunist thief.
- If you are unhappy at work, the best way to change this situation is to either change your mindset towards your job or get a new job. Don't blame your boss.

Here you can see cases of looking for positive outcomes from negative situations:

- The loss of a family member can cause distant relatives who haven't spoken for years to come together and reconnect.

- A health scare can make a person radically change their eating or lifestyle habits for the better.
- A failed project can lead you to planning better and ensuring you have adequate resources at your disposal next time.

The power in taking ownership and accountability is the control it gives you over your life. If you do not take ownership and you are not accountable, you relinquish this control to other people.

Playing it safe in life, by not taking any risks or not pushing yourself out of your comfort zone, is the enemy of progress and success. As John A. Shedd once noted. "A ship is safe in harbour, but that is not what ships are built for."

Dare to Set a New Standard

Prior to Sir Roger Bannister in 1954, no one had ever run a mile in four minutes or less. Six weeks later, John Landy, who had run with Bannister in Vancouver when Bannister had broken the record, also ran a sub four-minute mile. To date, at least 1,400 other people have beaten and even bettered this record.

Bannister believed that he was going to smash this artificial restrictive construct. By breaking the record, he had unleashed the shackles that had held back so many runners up until then; all of a sudden, the four-minute mile no longer seemed an impossible dream.

This is a perfect example of where humanity has benefited greatly from people pushing the boundaries. Quite often when one person achieves something, this sets a new benchmark, which then allows people to think (and believe) that a new standard is attainable.

As the great philosopher Socrates said, on realising ones' potential,

"No man has the right to be an amateur in the matter of physical training. It is a shame for a man to grow old without seeing the beauty and strength of which his body is capable."

Comfort Is the Enemy of Success

Are you comfortable? Do you receive monthly pay for your job and all is well, or do you feel that there is too much month at the end of your money?

Receiving your monthly pay can be a little like receiving a drug. You receive your 'hit' at the end of the month, you are happy, then you go out and treat yourself. Then, as the new month progresses, you see your bank balance rapidly reducing and you start feeling a little anxious and begin looking forward to the next pay day.

Are you cruising along in your career and all is well? You are neither pushed nor challenged and yet you know things are good, safe and comfortable. Although this doesn't necessarily sound like a bad thing, you are not pushing yourself to the next level. That next level might be getting the promotion you always wanted, going on a cruise around the world, or buying the home you always dreamed of.

Get comfortable with being uncomfortable.

The irony is that, with being comfortable, you feel content and have no real need to leave that place of comfort. To achieve your success, you will need to get comfortable with being uncomfortable.

Becoming successful invariably takes time, but you are a determined person. Therefore, with the right support and taking massive action, you will achieve whatever you set your mind to.

Most people dip their toes into the well of discomfort and rapidly pull out, since it's not necessarily a familiar or nice place to hang around. You are different, though. You will not only dip your toe in, you will learn to acknowledge that this will be the place where you will grow both as a human being by experiencing new things and also the place where your success becomes a reality.

As actress Andrea Vasiliou emphasised in Your Success Podcast episode 24, talking of the people that were on film set with her:

"The training really did push me to another level, a level which I never thought I was capable of achieving. You don't realise just how far you can push yourself physically and mentally, until you have no choice with a trainer on your back and a team to hold you accountable, so it's great to have that competitive spirit as well as having a great bunch of people to work with."

Remember: just because it is familiar and feels safe, it isn't always what is best for you and your success.

Risk vs Reward

With any decision, there is always a "risk factor" calculation that must be performed in your head. Is the potential reward that is linked to an activity worth the risk involved in the activity?

For taking more risk, there should be more reward, and if you can find something low risk that has a high potential reward, you are on to a winner!

We are not advocating recklessness with your decision making, but rather more controlled risk taking. No matter what area of your life you are considering making changes to, whether personal or business, make any changes in a controlled way.

There are varying levels of risks associated with different business models and careers. For example, you might sell your own brand in terms of being an actor, singer or influencer, which requires less start-up capital to get going than a business where you have to import goods from another country and pay for them before realising any profit. Starting a business where you buy property to sell or rent out will require more start-up capital, but you have a tangible asset at the end of it. However, the risks here could be volatility with the market price and the ability to rent the property.

Before you begin your new enterprise, consider whether you are ready to take on the additional risk, pressures and responsibilities that inevitably come when starting something new. The list below isn't a definitive list but should give you an overview of some of the things to consider when starting up new types of business.

Businesses Need Seed Capital

Most start-up businesses require an investment of seed capital in the beginning, but where does this come from? Of course, this all depends on how much your business plan dictates you require. As an aside, if you are not able to afford certain expertise at the very start, then you can either skill yourself up (which takes time) or outsource to other people on a part time basis. Outsourcing is discussed in more detail in Chapter 7 – Environment.

Where will the investment come from?

There are many different options available to you, with some of the most common ways listed below:

- Family;
- Friends;
- A bank loan;
- Credit cards;
- Crowd funding;
- Venture Capitalist investors.

What If Things Go Wrong?

How much risk are you willing to take on?

If you have borrowed seed capital, how do you plan on paying back your investors? Will it be a straight loan type arrangement, or perhaps the arrangement will be a profit share? However you decide to structure it, **always** write down on a piece of paper what the exact terms of the agreement are and ensure that this is signed by all parties involved.

This cannot be stressed enough as there have been plenty of perfectly good working relationships that have broken down because of what is called 'repayment amnesia', where one side forgets what was borrowed, or at what interest rate, or when it was agreed to be paid back. By writing it down, and having both sides sign the agreement, then there can be no doubt as to who owes what to whom and when it is due.

Hope for the Best, Plan for the Worst

How will you pay back the investor? Perhaps you have initially borrowed from family or friends because of their relationship and trust in you. The potential issue here is that you not only have the responsibility of returning their investment in full, but also the emotional burden should you not fulfil your obligations.

Always have a plan for how you intend to pay back the investor, but also have a plan B in case everything goes wrong. Worst-case scenario is that your new venture fails completely; how will you protect yourself? More importantly, how will you protect your investor?

It is not our intention to sound overly negative or cautious, but it is always best to be prepared when you meet a potential investor, as these questions will no doubt be some you will be faced with. You need to have given some thought to what you will say beforehand.

Do You Enjoy Your Success Now, or Reinvest It?

How many years of struggle will you endure before you start to realise your ambitions or see a reward? This is the age-old question. Do you continue ploughing in your time and money for something that you may not see a return in many years, if ever? There are no guarantees in life, so only you can decide how long you will continue before you enjoy the fruits of your labour.

You should always pay yourself, no matter how small the salary, as you will need to live, but also you should be remunerated for your hard work. If you pay yourself too much, especially at the start, you could leave the business under-capitalised which puts it at risk. Let's not forget Mr Tax Man who will want his pound of flesh at the end of the year, so always make sure you make sufficient provision to pay what is owed.

Reinvesting everything back into the business can really propel the business, but you also need to be paid for your efforts. Finding a balance between paying yourself and reinvesting in the business will take time, but it is certainly a wise thing to keep an eye on your long-term ambitions for the company as well as what you want in life.

Obsession vs balance is discussed in greater detail in Chapter 9 – Action.

As business turnaround expert Peter Hill said in Your Success Podcast episode 39:

"The person who says, "if only I earned £10k a year more, life would be easy" then they earn that money, buy a bigger car and go on a nicer holiday and repeat "if only I earned £10k more." I think a key measure of building wealth (not the only measure of success of course) is reinvesting returns today so that one day the investments will give you a higher rate of return than your income."

Just because you have received a pay rise (via your business or your job) and it is there to spend, doesn't always mean the correct thing to do is to spend the additional surplus money you have. People tend to live up to the income they receive and want the next best thing once they have become used to a certain standard of living, but is that always wise? Once they are living up to that standard, they will begin looking ahead and desiring newer, better things or experiences. Soon enough they will need an additional £10k per year just to maintain their new lifestyle.

By taking control and responsibility for your spending, you will have much great control over your life. Map out and plan your spending and what you need, then budget for the nice things so that you are not in the same position that you were when you needed £10k more per year to live a more comfortable life. Perhaps the best thing you could do with the surplus funds you have is to reinvest it in yourself, business or whatever your success plan needs to succeed.

Excuses

The journey to success is not an easy one, and there will be many obstacles along the way. However, it is important to not use these obstacles as reasons for stopping your progress towards success.

People make excuses when they are not taking ownership and accountability for their actions. As discussed earlier in this chapter, ownership and accountability are absolutely critical to taking control of your life; excuses have no place in your success journey.

If you are committed, you will find a way. If you are not committed and just interested, you will make an excuse. Below are some common excuses and how a different perspective on these situations can actually be a positive thing.

Excuse 1: I Am Too Old / I Am Too Young

Age is just a number and often used as an excuse for not acting. However, there are advantages in both whether you are younger or older:

Advantages of Starting When Older

Some of the advantages of making changes in your life to become the success that you always wanted in your more senior years are detailed below:

More experience - You are older, therefore by default you have more experience about the way the world works and that can be an advantage over your younger counterparts. You have the experience to know how to handle the different types of personalities that you will come across. You can potentially see bumps in the road earlier than someone younger and therefore be proactive about either side stepping them all together or putting plans in place to mitigate those issues.

Wider network - Your network of friends and acquaintances, from work and beyond, can be used to your advantage. So, when you plan to make changes in your life, you can rely on a much bigger pool of knowledge and talent to bounce ideas off or seek advice from.

More wealth - You might have accumulated a pot of wealth at this stage in life and could use that to supplement a pause in your existing career whilst you work out how to make your plan for success a reality. You could invest that pot into something that gives you passive income, so you can do what you truly love and still be aligned to your 'why' and vision of success.

Let's be honest here, you are likely to die sooner than your younger counterparts so if you are putting off becoming a success, now is the time to get a move on and do it!

Many great things have been achieved by older people. One example is Ray Kroc, who is responsible for developing McDonald's into what it is today. Kroc was born in 1902 in Illinois, United States, and was a businessman who turned the McDonald's restaurant into a national and then global franchise, in the process making it the most successful fast food company in the world.

He joined McDonald's aged 52 and rapidly expanded by opening/reforming restaurants across the United States. Kroc loved the founding brothers' idea of a clean and efficient business with everything standardised, so he rolled this model out across all restaurants with clear instructions on how to serve food the McDonald's way!

By the time Kroc died in 1984, the chain had 7,500 outlets in the United States and had expanded into 31 different countries. He passed away with a net worth was around $600 million – an incredible achievement for someone who started later in life.

Another example of someone who really set the standard for what an older person is capable of is King Leonidas of Sparta, Ancient Greece, born circa 540 BC.

Aged around 60, he led his elite 300 Spartan soldiers (with assistance from other Greeks) against unimaginable odds and for three days held back an invasion force of invading Persians, estimated to be in the region between 100,000 - 300,000 men! The Spartans were betrayed by a shepherd who told the Persians about a little-known track which led them behind the Spartans. The Spartans were eventually surrounded and fought to the last man, even fighting hand to hand in the end!

Word soon spread about the valiant Spartans sacrificing themselves giving time for Athens and Sparta to prepare for the upcoming onslaught, thus uniting Greece. Athens and Sparta were happiest when fighting each other, but the 300 Spartans' sacrifice helped unite the warring cities and defeat the Persian foe.

This stopped the expansion of the tyranny of Persia. If Greece had fallen, the invading Persians would have faced little opposition further west within Europe. If this had happened, then it is unlikely we would have democracy, science, certain schools of philosophy, and history as we know it today.

So, the next time you try and use age as an excuse, think back to King Leonidas leading his 300 men, having to brutally fight for three days to defend his country, and inspiring people over 2,000 years later!

Advantages of Starting When Younger

Let's look at the advantages of starting at a younger age.

Naivety - You are green, mean, and a little naive. You have a certain amount of naivety about you and haven't accepted society's limitations as your own; you dare to dream outside of the box, you can see the world differently and perhaps challenge the status quo.

Optimism - You haven't been corrupted by the world's cynicism yet and your blade hasn't been dulled by knock backs or people transposing their limiting beliefs onto you. You also have energy and time on your side. Creating your success will require lots of energy in order to achieve it. Thankfully, you will have this in abundance.

Time - Should you start something new and it does not work out, that's fine because you have time to start again (with the same or different mission), learn from the mistakes and avoid them the second time around.

Compounding - You also have the advantage of the compound effect having more time to help you, so you don't necessarily need to work as fast. A great example of compounding over time is billionaire investor and philanthropist Warren Buffet:

Buffet was born in 1930 in Omaha, United States, and is a legend when it comes to investing and creating wealth. He is widely regarded as the best investor of all time!

Buffet started at the age of five, selling lemonade outside his friend's house as there were more potential customers passing by compared to selling it outside his own home.

At age six, he purchased six packs of Coca Cola from his grandfather's grocery store for $0.25 and then sold them for $0.30, making a five-cent profit!

By the age of 11, he had made a total of $120 and naturally, after making an income, he had to file his first tax return and submitted it aged 14 for a total income of $592.50 for that year. Not bad for a 14-year-old!

Buffet continued investing and compounding his earnings and is now worth an estimated $80 billion!

Excuse 2: I Don't Have Enough Money to Get Started

Have you measured how much money you really need to implement your success plan, or has it always been a massive unknown quantity?

You probably need less than you think, and you can grow your business incrementally. After all, you don't need facilities or staff to serve 50,000 customers if you don't even have your first customer yet!

As mentioned earlier in the chapter, even if your success plan involves start-up capital, there are many sources of funding available, including:

- Borrowing from family and/or friends;
- Getting a loan from a bank;
- Crowdfunding;
- Angel investment (similar to Dragons' Den).

Note: Seek professional advice before borrowing any money and make sure all agreements are documented.

Excuse 3: I Don't Have Enough Time

You will make time, or you will make excuses. You might be saying, "well that's easy for you to say, I have a hard job and I never get any time to myself." We all get the same number of hours in a day, it's what you do with that time that matters.

The good news is that you can do certain things to free up more time for yourself so that you can focus on your success.

Auditing how your time is spent is a great way of mapping out 'exactly' what you get up to compared to what you 'think' you do. There might be some surprises in store for you.

- Is there a spare 30 minutes or an hour at night that you could use to work on your success plan instead of watching television?
- Instead of going to the pub, could you work on a marketing plan for your new business?
- Could you outsource some household jobs such as cleaning and shopping, to save you time so that you can work on yourself?

Time is never the issue: it is the prioritisation and allocation of time that is the issue. Think about time spent vs time invested. Once time is spent it is gone, whereas time invested repays many times over (e.g. time spent with your children and growing your business).

Excuse 4: I Wasn't Born a Success

Hopefully by now, you will see that nobody is born a success. Some people are born with a talent, some people are born into wealth and some people are born into environments that may be conducive to success. Despite all of this, nobody is born successful.

Success is something that has to be earned and worked hard for, and even if you are born into a good environment, you will still have to put the work in to become successful.

Anyone is capable of achieving success regardless of any actual or perceived barriers in their lives. You create your success with your friends, hard work, perseverance, determination, and all of the 10 traits listed within this book. Adhere to these traits and you will realise your success.

Regret

"You only live once" is a phrase used to represent making decisions based on wanting to experience all that life has to offer and not to hold back.

We do only live once, and it is important to make the most of our lives: both in terms of striving for success from a career or business point of view, and from the point of view of experiences and time spent with family and friends.

There have been several research studies looking to understand what people regret the most when lying on their death bed. Interestingly enough, no one mentioned working longer hours or needing more followers on a social media platform to feel fulfilled.

Research by Bronnie Ware (an Australian nurse who spent many years looking after elderly people) documented their dying wishes into a list of top 5 regrets:

"I wish I'd had the courage to live a life true to myself, not the life others expected of me."

This was the number one regret that most people had, and this is why at the start of this book it was emphasised how important it is to follow your vision and values as opposed to allowing others to impose their vision on you.

You are either living your vision by your own definition or living your life by someone else's vision.

"I wish I hadn't worked so hard."

Rather than working every hour of the day, missing your children growing up or sacrificing quality time with your partner or friends, create time to spend with them. Life will always be filled with opportunities and problems, but time spent with loved ones cannot be replaced.

Obsession versus balance – the ability to temper the obsession of achieving your success and have balance is a very important skill to have, as it will allow you to have more fun and be happier along the way to achieving your success. No-one wants to be miserable whilst working on their success journey. This balance is explored in more detail in Chapter 10 – Long Term Success.

"I wish I'd had the courage to express my feelings."

Suppressing your feelings and not expressing your true thoughts or intentions, bottling them up, was a big regret for people and even caused some of them to become ill.

Holding onto bitterness is like holding a burning piece of coal in your hand; in the end, only you are being burnt. If you are not happy with a situation, express your thoughts and you will probably feel happier for it, even if it results in having uncomfortable conversations.

"I wish I had stayed in touch with my friends."

Spending quality time with friends is often the first thing to be compromised when working on creating success. Maintaining friendships takes time but is definitely worthwhile if you can relax and create happy memories together. Ensure that you make time to spend time with your friends, even if your success plan is paused for a day or weekend. Everyone misses their friends when they are dying.

"I wish that I had let myself be happier."

Happiness is a choice, plain and simple. You control whether you are happy or not, but sadly not many people realise this until the very end of their lives.

Challenge yourself more and think long and hard about the following:

What do you regret and what would you want to not have to regret on your death bed?

You should always try to live a life without regrets. As Apple Inc. founder, Steve Jobs said,

"If today was the last day of your life, would you want to be doing what you are about to do today?"

How sad it is that some people prevent their talent or idea, which could change their own and other people's lives, from ever seeing the light of day! They have placed their idea on a pedestal and have artificially placed a restriction on achieving that goal.

You do not want to look back on your life with regret.

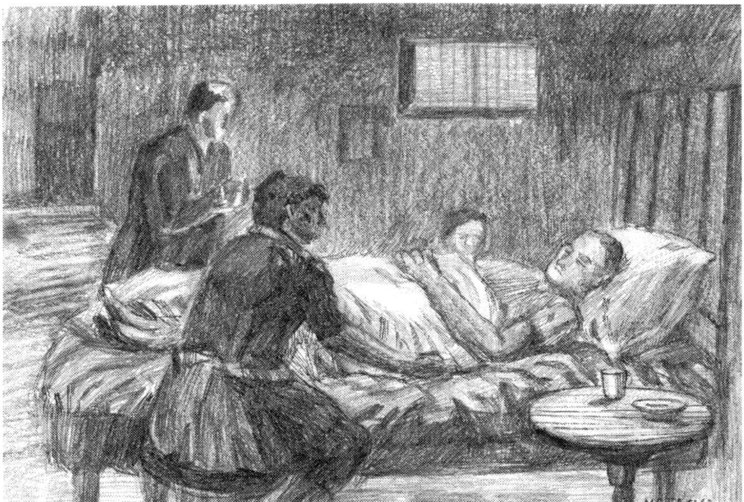

'If only' are the two saddest words in the English language, but they can easily be replaced by 'what if?' – it is up to you!

Summary

- You have to take ownership and responsibility for your own life. This gives you control over your destiny and is very empowering.
- Remove excuses from your vocabulary. If you are committed, you will find a way. If you aren't, you will find an excuse.
- Seed capital will be probably be required when starting your new venture. So, ensure you manage the risks by seeking professional advice and always write down anything of importance to avoid misunderstandings later on.
- Do not live with regret. You have one life and you owe it to yourself to create the best life you possibly can.

Action Steps

1. Write down your gifts and/ or the things that you have to offer to the world.
2. Write down one or two things that you always talk about doing but have never done (or told yourself you can't do).
3. Complete the Chapter 5 tasks in the Your Success Toolkit (available at www.yoursuccesspodcast.com/toolkit) including identifying and overcoming excuses.

Chapter 6

Fear and Limiting Beliefs

SUCCESS TRAIT 6:
Successful people do not let fear or limiting beliefs cripple them

The purpose of this chapter is to explore fear and limiting beliefs so that that you can identify, face, and overcome anything in your life that you are fearful of.

As this chapter will explore, fear is a natural phenomenon. It's a fundamental part of the survival mechanism that has kept the human race alive for so long. But when we talk about fear from a success point of view, it can be completely crippling to your success. This is because fear will stop you doing exactly what is required to progress and grow into the person you need to become to achieve the success you desire. Fear can be paralysing, and as described in Chapter 9 – Action, there is no progress without action. Being paralysed by fear is a guaranteed way to stay exactly where you are in your life.

Managing your fear will be one of the key drivers of your success and an ability to acknowledge when you are feeling fearful (and taking necessary precautions to reduce any associated risks), but pressing on anyway, will hugely increase your chances of success.

Fear is the expectation of a negative result, based on either:

- Your own past experience (e.g. you invested in property before and you lost money, so you expect that if you invest in property again, you will lose money);
- Someone else's experience (e.g. a friend went travelling to a certain country and was robbed, so you think that if you went to that country the same would happen to you). This can even be messages you get through the media. You don't have to know the person in question, fear is infectious, and you can adopt another persons' fear;
- An irrational fear based on neither of the above where neither you nor anyone you know have any experience of it, but you are still fearful: such as public speaking for the first time.

In all three of the above scenarios, you have no solid evidence of what the outcome will be.

Just because something negative happened before, doesn't mean that it will happen again.

There is a whole host of reasons for this: the timing is different, the people involved may be different, the surrounding circumstances may be different, and probably most obviously, you would have learnt lessons from the first negative experience either yourself or via the experience of another person.

Fear is often referred to as '**F**alse **E**xpectations **A**ppearing **R**eal'. In your mind, the negative outcome has already happened, even before you've taken any action, and this can be completely paralysing.

Fear Is Meant to Protect Us

Fear is actually a survival mechanism and originates from the area of the brain known as the limbic system (which is responsible for all emotions). When you feel fear (a perceived threat), your limbic system immediately reacts via your autonomic nervous system. This is known as the 'fight or flight' response.

To start tackling this, take small steps towards the thing you are fearful of. An easy example to mention here is the fear of spiders. A few easy steps to overcome a fear of spiders might include:

1. Start off by researching exactly what types of spiders are actually dangerous, and where in the world they live.
2. Set about finding somewhere you can get contact with a small spider that is not dangerous.
3. Handle the spider until you feel comfortable.
4. Work your way up to handling larger spiders, all the time safe in the knowledge that all of the spiders that you handle are not dangerous.

This is not to trivialise the fear of spiders – it is just to show a progression in incremental steps that would take you from one point to another.

Another fear might be a fear of job interviews, and this could well be based on a bad experience in the past where an interview went particularly badly. The way to conquer this fear might be:

1. Prepare for a fresh round of interviews, by doing some dummy interviews with a friend or family member.
2. Once you have gained some confidence, line up some interviews for jobs you don't really want that much. This way, if you don't get offered any of the jobs, you won't be disappointed. Remember to always ask for feedback and use this to perform better and better in each interview you have.
3. Once you have completed a few interviews and gained some confidence, move on to interviews for the jobs that you do want.

By the time you get to the interviews for the jobs you do want, you will have had so much practice, and will be so confident, that the fear will have subsided (or at least decreased dramatically)!

The fact is, failures and crises will happen if you are striving for success; you cannot be fearful of them. You need to be resilient enough to deal with them as they occur, and where possible, take the learnings from them forward into your future endeavours. Never let anything paralyse you from taking action towards your dreams.

Lack of Process or Understanding

In many circumstances, fear can be attributed to a lack of process, a lack of understanding, or a lack of practice.

Taking a flight on a plane can seem like a scary concept if you think about it. Flying through the air at hundreds of miles per hour in an aluminium can does seem scary, right? But, let's think about the millions of flights that have happened in the last 100 or so years, and think about the safety record of these flights. Let's think about the pre-flight, in-flight and post-flight checks. Think about the billions of pounds spent on aircraft technology. Think about the years of training that pilots immerse themselves in. Think about the black box data from the extremely rare occasions when planes do crash, and how this is shared between airlines and plane manufacturers to help improve the industry as a whole.

When you take these things into consideration, you start to get a more balanced view. Sure, there are risks in flying, the same way as there are risks when getting into a car, on a bicycle or even walking across the road! If you want to travel across the planet using a high-speed method of travel, then this might be expected.

In addition to a lack of understanding, a lack of process can also be a contributing factor to fear. Not knowing what happens and in what order can be crippling. An example here might be starting a new job. Contrast first day nerves with how you feel once you have been in the job for a year or two. All that has really happened is that you have learned the processes associated with the job and your confidence has grown as a result.

As David Thomas says in Your Success Podcast episode 12:

"'Glossophobia' – there's a word you've never heard of. That's the fear of public speaking and it is the number one social anxiety disorder, or number one fear. So, 10% of people have a massive fear. We're talking like pathological fear of speaking in public. The reason is because they don't have a process."

It is said that people rate the fear of public speaking higher than the fear of dying!

Everyone Begins Fearful

The thing to remember when you encounter fear or doubt is that everyone is, or has been, fearful of something in the past. Also, people who appear to be supremely confident can actually be fearful if you take them out of their comfort zone.

A world-famous public speaker who appears supremely confident and looks like they own the stage might be totally fearful if you put them on a football pitch, or in a corporate boardroom. At the same time, the skilled footballer who appears effortless and confident on the pitch, might be completely petrified if they have to give a speech on a stage in front of 10,000 people.

We tend to always look at the end result and compare ourselves to that. For example, we might look at someone confidently speaking on stage to 1,000 people and think that they are brave, or that they don't have any fear. What we neglect to remember, in this moment, is that the person we are watching has probably been speaking for five, ten, or even fifteen years and probably started off on much smaller stages, speaking to only a handful of people.

They were fearful then and will probably still get nervous and fearful before going on to a stage now. The person standing on the stage is not superhuman. They feel fear, the only difference in them is that they feel this fear and use the adrenaline it releases as a source of energy to go out and deliver their message to the world.

"Head In The Sand" Syndrome

Some of the most highly successful business people have woken up in the dead of night and experienced fear or uncertainty. The key is they did not allow fear to paralyse them into inaction.

You might wake up feeling dread, but even if you are feeling this focus on the next steps and tackle the hardest problems head on. Do not bury your head in the sand as an emu does; problems do not just disappear and will in fact probably get worse as a result of your inaction.

Remember that a problem shared is a problem halved. Try sharing the problem with your partner, closest friends, or mentor, as this will do two things:

1. Firstly, you will have unburdened yourself slightly by allowing the problem to escape from the confines of your own mind. Often keeping the problems to yourself can amplify a simple problem many times over, making a mountain out of a molehill. The relief created by unburdening yourself could be massive.
2. Secondly, the person you voice the problem to could offer a completely different perspective. This could lead to a solution being presented which you did not consider or did not allow yourself to see. Sometimes the solution is right in front of us; we just need someone to lift the veil of fog covering our worried eyes.

Fear as a Motivator

Fear can also be a great stimulus. Often, it can tell us exactly what we need to do to grow, whether it may be moving to the next level, or pushing us outside of our comfort zone.

Something you have been fearful of for years may have been preventing you from taking that next step in your life. Breaking through the fear can be the revelation that opens up new opportunities for you. Imagine someone scared of flying who finally gets on a plane and discovers it's not that bad and that their fear was unfounded. The whole world has opened up to them!

Should you be in a position where you have a family to feed and you have no other income, then the fear of your family going hungry can be a great stimulus to driving you forward and out of a bad situation. Fear shouldn't always be treated as a negative thing as it can drive you to new heights and uncharted territory.

Limiting Beliefs

Limiting beliefs are beliefs about yourself which hold you back, even though you often have no evidence to support them.

This is probably the most common objection but is seldom voiced out loud initially. This limiting belief can be crippling as you set the barriers to your own achievements. Why not tear down those barriers? Doing so may force yourself to feel new experiences and allow yourself to become successful.

The lack of confidence is no small matter to overcome, but also not an insurmountable feat.

An elephant which was tied to a strong post as a calf, would have struggled to pull away and escape for freedom. The link between the post and not being able to escape has been forged in its mind and has creating a limiting belief. Fast forward to now, into adulthood, the elephant still holds onto the same limiting belief that it couldn't pull away from the post. In reality, it could leave whenever it chose to.

The reason why limiting beliefs are so bad for you, is because they completely block any attempt to try new things that they relate to. For example, a limiting belief about your ability to complete a job role in a more senior position will prevent you from even applying for that job, or speaking with your manager to explore the possibility.

You will never know the outcome unless you try. Even if you applied for the job and didn't get it, at least you would have feedback on why you were unsuccessful. Maybe you need one more year of experience, or maybe you need to take a certain professional qualification and then you could return and apply for the position at a later date. But the limiting belief would prevent you from applying for the job in the first place.

In these situations, it is best to ask, "what's the worst that could happen?" In most cases, the worst-case scenario may be a bit of embarrassment (which may not even happen), but the opportunity is so great, and the upsides are so plentiful.

Why do people rarely ask for a massive pay rise, say jumping from £25,000 to £50,000? The answer is that they probably wouldn't get it even if they asked for it. Hello, limiting belief. Ironically, most people would not consider a pay reduction. It is funny how people limit their pay rises to small increments but will not budge with a reduction.

Give Yourself Permission to Succeed

Quite often the block between where you are now and where you want to be is to be found inside your own head. When faced with a new challenge or a dream that they want to achieve, people will often feel excited at the prospect of something new. Then a little voice in their head tells them to "hold back", "play it safe", "this is for other people", "know your station", and so on.

If you don't start off with a belief in your own ability, why would anyone else believe in you? They have their own problems to deal with and their own lives to live. It has to start with you. When you believe in yourself with such supreme confidence, others will feel this energy and be drawn to you. If it helps, look at it as your obligation to give yourself permission to succeed in order to force other people around you to 'level up' their own lives and their own self-belief.

Let go of the baggage of doubt!

Fear of What Other People Think

Worrying and being scared of what other people think of you is a guaranteed way to throttle your own success. People will always judge you, whether you are achieving great things or not.

Why let them dictate your life? Who are they to judge you for stepping outside of your comfort zone, for going outside of what is accepted as 'average' or 'normal'? Why not give something new a try?

Others will judge you through the prism of their own experience; if they have failed at something in their life, that you are now trying, they will project their bad experience of this on to you.

The hardest thing to deal with, however, is when your closest friends or family are being negative towards you and your plans. It is much easier to deal with negative comments or people projecting their own fears on to you when they are online, or from people you see relatively infrequently. The hardest thing to deal with is the consistent voices of your closest friends and family, chipping away at your dreams and grinding you down, just because they have had a bad experience or don't understand what you are doing.

That is not to say that your friends and family will necessarily react in this way, but if they do, know that (like your own body's survival mechanism) they are usually looking out for you and trying to protect you. Likely, they don't fully understand what you are doing. So, maybe sitting down with them and explaining both what it is you are doing and also how much it means to you will help them to feel more comfortable supporting you.

But, even if they don't come around to the idea, don't let this prevent you from doing what you want to do. Ultimately, it's your life and in fact you are doing a disservice to them by holding back on your dreams. The reason for this is that if you are unfulfilled because you have been put off by your partner (for example) exploring your passion or your dreams, this will lead to you resenting them for preventing you from doing so. This will ultimately result in arguments and ill-feeling in the relationship. Happiness has to start with you being in a place where you feel fulfilled and satisfied.

Fear of Rejection

The word 'no'.

Just two letters, and yet, what a powerful and sometimes crippling word it is. It sounds like such a final word and perhaps you have no come back, or plan B should someone deny you with the word 'no'.

Perhaps you need to reframe the word 'no' with, 'no, for now'. In sales, or business, no doesn't mean no – it often just means not now.

As Richard Fenton and Andrea Waltz discuss in their book, "Go for 'no'! 'Yes' is the destination, 'no' is how you get there", we need to seek out 'no's' in life, as this is the route to success. For example, in sales, you might need to get 100 'no's' before you get a 'yes', so get out there and start racking up those 'no's'.

Fenton and Waltz also mention, when all is said and done, that no one will remember your failures – they will just remember your successes. Like the hit artist who has released some poorly-received pop songs; people only remember the popular ones. Or the author who has a bestselling book, but if you look closely you can see they published some less popular books previously but all anyone talks about is their bestseller.

Remember: the market decides, not you, so do not let this cripple you into inaction. See Chapter 9 for more on taking massive action and being prolific, not perfect!

'No's' mean you can move on to speaking to someone who will actually be interested in what you have to offer. Alternatively, it gives you the exact feedback you need to be able to improve your offering and return to that previous customer or client and deliver something that garners a 'YES'.

Fear of Failure

We all want to be successful, whatever that means to you. Failure is the opposite of success, so by definition we do not want to fail. However, as with the previous fears mentioned in this chapter, fearing failure will prevent you from pursuing new ideas and progressing towards your vision of success.

Whilst you don't want to aim to fail, failure can be an important part of your journey. As discussed in Chapter 3 – Constant Learning and Growth, failure can be a valuable asset if the learnings from it are taken to improve, grow and move forward.

In most cases, fear of failure is actually a fear of what other people will think of you if you fail, and as discussed in this chapter, it doesn't matter what other people think; you need to live life on your terms and not be held back by other people's opinions. Find that courage within you to smash through your fears. It will be hard, and it takes valour, but what a rush when you finally do it. What are you scared of? Who could help you along this journey? Why not speak with people who have already done what you fear and ask them how they did it?

Summary

- Fear is an emotion that can be managed and reduced by taking small steps towards the very thing you are afraid of.
- Everyone is, or has been, fearful of something at some point in their life. There is nothing to be ashamed of in being fearful. Even people who appear supremely confident and scared of nothing, will be fearful when placed outside of their comfort zone. Get comfortable with being uncomfortable.
- Although scary, ironically, all of the growth occurs outside of your comfort zone, and when you feel fear, that is probably where you need to be heading to experience growth and move to the next level of success. Doors will open if you embrace the fear.
- Limiting beliefs are beliefs that you hold about yourself, which hold you back, even though you often have no evidence to support the beliefs. Limiting beliefs will prevent you from growing in your professional and personal life and are extremely poisonous. Always ask yourself "what is the worst that could happen?", embrace the fear, and remove those limiting beliefs.
- Do not be scared of hearing a 'no' – use it to your advantage.

Action Steps

1. Write down five fears or limiting beliefs that you think are holding you back.
2. For each one, write down two things that you could do to move towards conquering the fear. For example, if one of the fears/limiting beliefs is a fear of job interviews, schedule a mock interview with a trusted friend or family member.
3. Complete the Chapter 6 tasks in the Your Success Toolkit (available at www.yoursuccesspodcast.com/toolkit).

Chapter 7

Environment

SUCCESS TRAIT 7:
Successful people control
their external environment

This chapter explores the importance of the environment for your success and gives you ways in which, through small changes, you can start to enhance your environment and massively increase your chances of success.

The term 'environment' is used to describe where you live, where you work, who you interact with, what you consume (both into your stomach and your brain), who your friends are, who you spend time with, and what you do in your spare time.

Our environment has such a powerful effect upon us because we have to adapt to our environment to survive. Let's consider two identical Hydrangeas, planted in soil with differing pH levels, and how they grow flowers of different colours.

A Hydrangea planted in the more acidic soil will turn a deeper shade of blue, whereas a Hydrangea planted in more alkaline soil will produce a deep pink flower. This is as a result of their environment. Like the Hydrangea, we are just as influenced by our surroundings. Plant a human in a toxic environment and their progress is unlikely to be as quick or progressive as someone who has been nurtured in a positive environment.

When we talk about 'environment', most people think "well I'm not in control of my environment, I live where I live, if it rains, it rains, I can't control who my friends and family are and there aren't any healthy eating options for lunch near my work place", and so on.

The problem with thinking in this way, is that it relinquishes control of your entire life to other people and to other companies. Why should fast food chains determine what you eat? Why should your friends at the pub guilt trip you into consuming 10 pints of beer a week?

Here are a few quick changes you could make to help improve your environment:

- Tired of eating unhealthily at lunchtimes? Plan and prepare healthy packed lunches.

- Tired of drinking too much alcohol? Spend time with friends who don't drink as much.
- Tired of seeing negative news on the TV? Watch something else (or switch off the TV altogether).
- Tired of it raining all the time? Move to somewhere with less annual rainfall. Better still, create a weather control system – now that is a sure-fire way of becoming a success!

The point here is that you are in control!

As entrepreneur and author Rob Moore stated in Your Success Podcast episode 45:

"[In] Every story, when you go back you see that they've been in a good environment. In Matthew Syed's case [the former English and Commonwealth champion table tennis player], all the best table tennis champions were on his street, the best coaches were in his town. That is not genetic, that's environment and sometimes you're lucky to be born into that environment, but you still have to make the best of what you've got."

Habits and paradigms are also explored as they control your day to day life, often without you being consciously aware of them.

In terms of your environment, let's begin by examining the most prevalent influence on your environment: people.

People

'People' are the area of your life in which you can make the biggest improvements in terms of environment. Without realising it, on a daily basis, we are hugely influenced by the people we spend time with. As world famous motivational speaker Jim Rohn famously said, "you are the average of the five people you spend the most time with." This encompasses everything from health and wellbeing, your view of the world, income, net worth and so on.

Have you ever felt that, after speaking to someone who has a very cynical, negative view of the world, you find yourself feeling more negative? Or on the positive side, have you ever spent time with someone with good eating and exercise habits who has inspired you to go for that jog, or swap that plate of chips for a salad? It's infectious!

Serial entrepreneur and author John Lamerton described the effect that your environment can have on you in Your Success Podcast, episode 38:

"The people you surround yourself with, what you put into your ears, your eyes, and your mouth, dictates the life you've got. So, surround yourself with positive people, surround yourself with good personal development. Listen to a podcast like this, watch YouTube videos, read books. Get yourself educated, get your environment right so that it actually supports you. If the five people you hang around with are all losers who hate themselves, guess what? You're going to hate yourself too."

Teamwork makes the dream work! No astronaut ever went into space because of their solo effort. There is always a team of thousands of highly trained professionals working behind the scenes, working tirelessly for one common purpose: placing the astronaut high above our heads. The flight of the astronaut is the culmination of decades of combined effort between the thousands of engineers, technicians, and construction workers. Imagine what you could do with thousands of employees all working towards achieving your vision. It isn't easy to embark on this journey alone but with help, the journey could be a lot easier, a lot more fun and probably a lot more productive. Remember, two heads are better than one.

There are several different ways you can work with and get support from others to arrive at your success, such as:

- Business partners;
- Employees;
- Outsourcers;

- Mentors/Coaches.

Working with people in these roles is explored below.

Business Partners

Often, bouncing ideas backwards and forwards with a business partner can yield great results, and better results compared to flying solo.

Care must be exercised when finding business partners. Don't rush out and find a business partner as you may not need one yet, or at all, but having a close confidant to help bounce ideas off is important. When choosing business partners, it is vital to find people with different skillsets, and with a vision and values that are aligned with our own.

Ideally, you want to find someone with different skill sets so that you do not tread on each other's toes, however it is important for you to have an aligned vision and values for where you are taking the company. Otherwise, you will not be able to reach agreement on important strategic decisions.

You also need to factor in that the relationship must be equitable and sustainable from the start. These are very subjective factors and keeping the lines of communication open between partners is essential to prevent the relationship breaking down.

Remember that if you want to go fast, go alone. If you want to go far, then go together.

It is rare that successful people have done it on their own. Below are a couple of examples of highly successful people who had a partner(s) and achieved great things.

1. Steve Jobs and Steve Wozniak (Apple Inc.)

There are few people on this planet who have not heard of Apple. It all started in a garage with the two Steves working together on designing the 'Apple I' computer. This started a revolution in the computing world and led to many other great successes together. Jobs had great marketing and showmanship skills and was able to present Apple devices to audiences that broke new ground and set the standard for the build-up of anticipation before a product launch. Wozniak was a technical genius in designing the Apple I and II computers, but he was not a showman like Jobs. Because of this combination of their two strengths we ended up with a trillion-dollar company named Apple.

2. Kirk, Spock, and McCoy (Crew of the USS Enterprise, Star Trek - TV series)

This is a great example of opposing skillsets working perfectly when combined. When you are busy being the Captain of the Starship Enterprise, you need a strong partnership.

Spock (First Officer) is a highly logical Vulcan who would see situations in a cold and reasoned manner, seldom letting emotions cloud his judgement or decision-making. Then we have Dr McCoy (ship's physician), an emotionally charged individual who frequently antagonised Spock as he could not understand his total logical attitude to human problems.

Sat there in the middle was Captain Kirk. Kirk was an archetypical action hero, who would use his fists as often as sound reasoning when dealing with adversaries. To Kirk's left was McCoy who would reason out the morals and ethics in a dilemma, and to Kirk's right was Spock, who would argue what the most logical thing to do in the situation. Kirk would listen to both sides and then come to a balanced conclusion leading to a well thought out solution based upon his own reasoning and logic and taking into account all the information and evidence he received from his two colleagues. Usually, he was right.

This is a great example of where a partnership can do well by having differing viewpoints showing you the multiple sides of an argument. As the leader, you can then make a reasoned and well-considered choice drawing from different skillsets and opinions.

Honesty Hour

The most common reason for a business partnership disintegrating is the breakdown of trust. With partnerships, there are times when there will be a perception from one side of the partnership that perhaps the other partner is not pulling their weight. Over time, this generates resentment, a small issue will blow up, and the response will be completely out of proportion. Think of a shaken-up cola bottle exploding once the lid pops off.

In any working relationship, there will be times where one partner is distracted and not pulling their weight, or the other partner will at least perceive that to be true. Maybe you need to sit down with your partner and air out those differences; the key here is not to just make it a session all about perceived slights. Instead, the purpose is to raise any queries about differing expectations and performance early on and discuss them, showing gratitude for the strengths and values that make the relationship work. Be prepared to listen not just talk. Despite popular belief it is not just other people who don't like criticism, it can also be hard for us to accept it too. The aim is information gathering and constructive feedback.

An easy way to quickly address issues before they become real problems, is to meet with your business partner every month, perhaps over a drink to air out any issues, and making it clear that any problems can be aired without fear. This promotes an atmosphere of honesty and allows for perceived slights to be resolved before they affect the operation of your business, or even worse, create an enemy out of your partner.

Quite often, what you perceived to be your partner not working as hard as you (in your mind) is often wrong and they will tell you what is really going on. Honesty Hour is the perfect place to do this.

As entrepreneur and author Rob Moore stated in Your Success Podcast episode 45, speaking of his business partner Mark Homer:

"I trust him, and he trusts me, and that it is worth so much more than anything else really. We cut a deal in the early days where anything he wants to do, fine, he has to cut me in 50%. The other way around also stands. I see a lot of people in partnerships, and instead of looking at all the things their partner brings, they often think "they're not working very hard. They're not really delivering, and I'm frustrated with them. We measure people on our values, I shouldn't be measuring him on my values, I should be measuring him on his own values. Try being a good partner rather than trying to squeeze your partner into how you want them to be."

Employees

What skills do you possess? More importantly, what skills are you missing or are not very good at? Perhaps you hate certain aspects of business, such as bookkeeping. This is where you need to find someone to start plugging these gaps. Perhaps you need someone great at tax strategy, maybe it is law you are unsure about or financing. It may be that systems and operations leave you puzzled.

"I am just starting up and I can't afford any members of staff" is a common cry from the solopreneur. If you are unable to afford a full-time member of staff initially, then why not consider employing them on a part-time basis? You could have multiple part-time personnel helping you grow your business until you are at a place where you can employ some people on a full-time basis.

The key with employees is to ensure that they understand and have bought in to the vision for the company and work according to the values of the company. This way, you as the company owner can influence the way the business acts without having to micromanage the team.

Outsourcers

From a business point of view, it is always good advice to outsource tasks that don't inspire you to employees, subcontractors, or business partners. There are books which say, "know your worth per hour and outsource everything." For the most part, this is true. It is only by growing as a person and moving up to higher and higher value tasks that you grow your business, income, and worth.

If you can pay someone £8 per hour to do something you don't enjoy, which also frees up your time to either work (assuming you earn more than £8 per hour), or build your business, this is a good idea.

But what if you love gardening, or cleaning? What if you really enjoy number-crunching? Surely the key to a fulfilled life is to keep hold of the things that make you happy? Before you outsource everything, it is also wise to know a little about each task you are outsourcing. Otherwise, how will you be able to measure and create meaningful Key Performance Indicators (KPIs) without knowing what is involved in the running of the outsourced task?

Key Performance Indicators are tangible, measurable targets that you can use to communicate what 'good performance' looks like to an employee, outsourcer, or business partner. An example of a KPI in a business might be the number of sales in a day, or the number of 5-star customer reviews. In a personal capacity, a KPI could be number of hours dedicated to spending quality time with your children, or the number of times you have met up with friends in a month.

A prime, real-life example of doing what you enjoy and not necessarily outsourcing everything, is a young property development couple. Let's call them Becky and Phil.

Becky and Phil have grown their property development and investment business over the past few years, to a point where they conservatively have £5,000,000 worth of property and income in excess of £100,000 per year. This puts their 'hourly rate' at somewhere around £48 per hour each.

As they take on new property development projects, they can (and should, in theory) pay someone more junior (but with adequate experience) maybe £10-£15 per hour to conduct viewings for new potential projects. Becky and Phil have worked hard to develop processes, procedures, and checklists to allow someone to complete this task.

But there is one thing to consider: Becky and Phil love doing new property viewings. It reminds them of when they first started out in property together. Simply put, they love brainstorming ideas for layouts and interior designs.

So, they outsource the initial viewing to their viewings manager, whom they pay £12 per hour. He filters out all of the less desirable properties, then passes the information on to Becky and Phil to complete the second viewing.

They have created a win-win scenario whereby they still get to do what they love, but the business continues to grow as they are valuing their self-worth.

Outsourcers (or sub-contractors) are great because you get a similar benefit to employees, but without the overheads and responsibilities you have as an employer (such as sick pay, holiday pay, and so on). Bear in mind that outsourcers are self-employed and as such can have as many other clients as they like. So, being clear with KPIs and deadlines, and having crystal clear how-to guides, is important.

The Man Who Outsourced His Whole Job!

This is a case of someone who outsourced his entire job whilst working for a company. Whilst his employer was certainly not happy with this (and fired him for it), you have to admire his outsourcing abilities.

The employee was a software developer for a US-based company who outsourced his work to China. He would spend his days browsing the internet and watching YouTube videos instead. He reportedly paid only a fifth of his six-figure salary to his outsourcers, so in essence he was paid to browse the internet all day!

Author, publisher, and outsourcing expert, Rick McMunn, stated in Your Success Podcast episode 52:

"What I love about outsourcing is that you can outsource jobs and it doesn't matter how small or big you are as a business; it works well for everybody. If I was starting out now I would use outsourcers to help me scale up the business as I go along.

Some people say you must have hundreds and hundreds of outsourcers that you use. I don't, I have a small group of people that I use, and they are fortunate because I literally spend hundreds and thousands of pounds with them! And it is great for me because they are tried and tested, I trust them and more often than not, I wake up in the morning and the job is done, which is brilliant, so it works really well."

Here are some examples of the types of tasks you could outsource:

- Bookkeeping.
- Editing of a book.
- Designing branding.
- Finding investment properties.
- Answering company phone calls.
- Growing your social media influence.
- Compiling data on current market trends.

There is a whole world out there where you can find jobs to be outsourced. If you get it right and work well with an outsourcer, you will be surprised by how much time it frees up for you to focus your attention on other high-level income generating activities within your business.

Mentors/Coaches

When embarking on your success journey it is important to find someone who has already accomplished what you are seeking to achieve and ask for their opinion on matters. Perhaps you would like to formalise this mentorship and pay for access to their time and knowledge, or maybe it is their network you would like access to.

This has helped many successful people out there. Finding the right mentor or coach can really accelerate your journey. A good mentor will push you well and truly out of your comfort zone.

There is definitely a place for well-informed and experienced individuals who offer their knowledge and guidance for free. Be careful with 'free' though, as free advice is often worth how much you paid for it!

It is quite common to have more than one mentor for different aspects of your life. For example, a business mentor is unlikely to help you get the six pack you have always wanted, and a fitness coach is equally unlikely going to help you put together a successful business plan.

How do you find a mentor or a coach? The questions to ask yourself when searching for a mentor or coach are:

- Has this person achieved what you are looking to achieve?
- Does this person have a demonstrable track record of what they claim to have achieved?
- After talking with them, do you feel inspired and do you think this person shares the same values as you?

Often people are put off by the high price a mentor can charge. But the question you have to ask yourself is how quickly can you make that money back with their guidance and advice, and how much are you leaving on the table by not paying for their help?

You will probably achieve your success given enough time and setbacks, but how much quicker could you achieve your success with their help?

Your Inner Circle

Indirectly and almost insidiously, you begin to inherit the behaviours and outlook of your circle of friends. That is why it is important to surround yourself with positive people who are happy to give constructive feedback. No-one wants to be surrounded by 'yes people' who never provide criticism, but equally you do not want to be surrounded by nay-sayers. Striking a balance between the two is key.

We are not saying you need to be ruled by committee: many an amazing project has been watered down by appeasing everyone in the committee. Sometimes, superstars have such a burning desire within them, that nothing will stop them from achieving whatever they set their minds to.

Let us look at an example of where a friend's lifestyle can have a direct impact on your success plan.

The Mate Down the Pub

Imagine that you have a friend in your circle called Steve. You meet Steve for a drink three times a week. Steve has a low paid job and likes to drink a lot, but he is a great laugh and you have been friends since school.

He has no aspirations to improve his life and is happy with his lot. Most importantly for you starting out with your success plan, is that he is very critical of new ideas, especially ideas that might disrupt his routine with you. Let us say your success plan is setting up a new gym that caters for healthy living, with the plan being to expand and create a chain of similar gyms. Is Steve likely to support your idea of wanting to pursue your success and offer support? Probably not.

Is this because your friend consciously does not want the best for you or is being malicious? No, often it is the fear of a change in the comfortable relationship with you. People can react strangely when new ideas or disruption to an existing routine are presented to them. Steve is not looking at your success plan and its great potential, but trying to keep you safe from harm as new ideas bring risks and both of you would be out of your comfort zones.

The difference here is that you are comfortable with being uncomfortable and most importantly, you have followed the guidance in earlier chapters on how to create your success plan. The ironic thing is when you become successful and complete your success plan, your friends might ask you for advice on how to turn their own lives around. Of course, you will give them inspiration and advice – as well as telling them to buy this book!

Ask yourself this: are you surrounded by five positive and supportive people who will keep you accountable and offer to support you when you embark on your success journey?

If not, perhaps it is time to find a more positive support circle. We are not advocating that you cut ties with your circle of friends, but maybe moderate the time spent with them and perhaps spend more time with people who inspire and support your ideas. There is every chance that, as your success grows, this will happen naturally.

Don't Be a Crab

Avoid people with 'crab mentality', as in 'if I can't have it, neither can you'.

With several crabs in a bucket, some of them could easily get out. However, as they fight and pull each other back, they prevent each other from escaping.

Some people, out of envy, spite, or more likely their own personal fear of growth when seeing someone venturing outside of their comfort zone, will try to hold them back if it looks like they are trying to achieve more than the average of the group. Avoid people with this mentality at all costs.

Enhancing Your Environment

"Great minds discuss ideas; average minds discuss events; small minds discuss people." - Henry Thomas Buckle.

The main objection people can have with changing their environment is that they can't change their family and leave behind the friends that they have grown up with or known for years (or decades). However, this is a misconception: completely cutting all negative people out of your life is not necessarily the correct advice to follow.

Below are some tips that can help you enhance your environment:

- Spend *less* time with friends and family whom you think are negative or holding you back. When you are with them, focus the conversation on the things they add to your life (for example discussing sports, children, food, or cars). Avoid talking about aspirational plans and ideas if they are consistently negative towards these. Let your results do the talking. We all have friends who we can spend a couple of hours with and after that, conversation turns stale and you know it is time to depart. Why stay there any longer? Set in your mind a rough schedule when spending time with friends for whom you know that there needs to be a time limit. Decide on who are one-hour friends, half-a-day friends, two-day friends, and so on.

- Join networking groups and online forums where the focus is on positive action-taking and where you will be supported in your ideas.
- Get a mentor/mentors who will help you along the way in your specific niche. They should be 'ahead' of you in the journey and will therefore be able to give you positive advice, which is grounded in reality.
- Plan your days. This includes planning work and planning meals (meal prep at home or planning where you can buy food that meets your vision for your health and wellbeing). This also includes planning exercise and where possible completing this in the morning when you have greater willpower reserves (remember - no one is going to invite you for a beer in the morning!)
- Start reducing your consumption of the tabloid media. Remember that their agenda is to sell newspapers and get viewers for their news programmes and hits on their website, to be able to sell advertising space. If you need to be up to date on current affairs for your job or business, carefully curate your media consumption/notifications/bookmarks on your computer and set time limits on how much time you will spend digesting their articles. Don't fill your brain with inconsequential rubbish, you are better than that: you deserve great brain food! Read a motivational or personal development book instead. We promise you that you will get a much better return on investment for your time.

Dealing with Haters

If you don't have haters, you are not making enough of an impact.

Haters are people who, despite your best efforts to deliver an excellent service, be nice to people, have empathy for other peoples' situations, and generally try to do good in the world, will tear into you, usually in a public forum whilst hiding behind a keyboard – the "keyboard warrior".

The important things to remember are:

1) People who hate others for no legitimate reason are usually saying a lot more about their own character than they are about yours. They may have been hurt in the past or have some emotional baggage and for some reason you trigger that emotion or memory. Remember it's not personal and it is more about them and their issues rather than a direct reflection of your product or service offering to the world.

2) You want to polarise opinion, and you need to accept that you will not be liked by everyone. By polarising opinion and having some raving fans and some haters, you will attract people who are aligned to your values and put off those who are not. This is good because you want your following, fans, and customers to be aligned with what you are about as they are much more likely to get value from what you are doing. By playing safe in the middle ground, you might spare yourself from having any haters, but this will come at the cost by not attracting anyone to you or your brand who is a true authentic fan and excited by what you are doing. The sooner you accept that you will always have some haters, the happier and calmer you will be.

3) The best way to silence haters is by being successful. Don't retaliate as this will just spur them on and give them more energy. Thank them for taking the time to respond to you, and move on. Remember to listen to legitimate criticism because not everyone will want to tear you down, they might simply want to give you some good feedback, even if it is not what you want to hear. Focus your energy and resources on positive, supportive people who are aligned

to what you believe in and let your success do the talking!

The above is easier said than done and needs to be practised. Celebrities frequently come out and say they have 10,000 great, positive comments on a piece of content they put out on social media, but they feel down when they see one or two nasty comments.

As absurd as this may sound, until you have experienced it, you can't know what it feels like. The key thing here is to either ignore the hate completely, or if the haters are unavoidable, ensure you balance it out with supportive, positive comments. Remember, most of these keyboard warriors would never say anything to your face and are much less vocal or courageous when their keyboard 'safety blanket' is removed.

Let Them Chew Wasps in the Shade of Your Success

By the very nature of what you are doing, there will always be someone who does not approve, like, or understand what you are doing. Thank them for their comments and move on. Remember, if you have haters, you are making an impact in the world. Therefore, if you do not have any haters at the moment, what are you waiting for? Get out there and start making more of an impact!

Remember, the best revenge on negative people is to do well. Haters are your motivators!

Changing Habits and Paradigms

Habits are regular actions we take, without really realising it, and for the most part they help us live a safe and enjoyable life. Examples of helpful habits include stopping at a road to check for traffic, driving a car, or brushing your teeth. Generally speaking, these things don't consume too much brain power. This is because the sub-conscious part of our brain has evolved to control these things, and it's one of the reasons humans can handle a multitude of tasks with ease.

However, negative habits can form just as easily as positive ones – having a cigarette when you feel stressed, having some chocolate after dinner, or snoozing your alarm for an hour before getting up. The brain thinks that these habits are helping us, because without knowing, we have trained it to think this and associate X with Y. For example, to associate having a cigarette with feeling calm and relaxed, or to associate having some chocolate with feeling satiated.

Paradigms are the way in which we view and make sense of a complex world. They are the mental models we build and associations we make that contextualise people, events, and places. Think of paradigms like computer programming. Paradigms control us, and again are hugely influenced by the people we spend time with and the information we consume (from friends, family, colleagues, the media, and so on).

An example of a paradigm might be 'rich people are evil', 'certain foods are appropriate for breakfast', or 'the earth is round'.

Whilst the earth being round is a scientifically provable fact (although some people still believe otherwise!) the other two examples above would divide opinion, depending on where you grew up, what your education was like, who your family was, and what you have experienced throughout your life.

The point here is that we are sub-consciously programmed to believe certain things and call them our own opinions – so we need to exercise caution about where this information is coming from!

We should always look to experts (and a variety of experts so we don't just get a one-sided view) to give us advice on re-programming negative paradigms. Always seeking opinions or facts that support your position is called confirmation bias, and can blinker your view as to what is actually happening. Having a balanced and non-biased view of facts can greatly enhance your reasoning and give you the ability to view situations in a calm and informed manner.

For example:

- Go to a nutritionist for advice on the best foods to eat and at what times of the day, especially if your success involves losing weight or maintaining a healthy lifestyle;
- Go to a personal trainer for advice and to hold you accountable if you have specific fitness goals;
- Speak to a cross-section of wealthy and poor people to work out for yourself if rich people truly are evil;
- Speak to people with disabilities who have achieved great things to work out what is possible in life if you have a disability.

You get what you tolerate in life, and if you spend time with people with low expectations, you will lower your expectations and standards for your own life. Set your own high standards for income, set standards for professionalism, set standards for health and wellbeing, set standards for the amount of time you spend with your family, and watch out for the nay-sayers or the negative people in your life who question these changes.

Setting standards is even more important if you have a team (or children) as what you consider to be acceptable behaviour will be modelled by them. For employees and children, their biggest role models are their boss(es) and their parents, respectively. For example, if you arrive late to meetings in your business, your employees will also believe it is acceptable to turn up late to meetings. Likewise, a child will inherit mannerisms from their parents. Should a parent not make a habit of being polite, then the child is also likely not to be polite to others.

Planning

Planning is an important part of habit-forming and paradigm-shifting.

You may know that a junk-food meal every day is probably not going to help you achieve your fitness goals, but if you don't make alternative plans, you may leave yourself with no choice. It has been proven that willpower is a finite resource and decreases throughout the day. So, even a day where you start off thinking 'I'm not going to eat anything unhealthy today or have any cigarettes / alcohol / caffeine', may end in you binging on one or more of these.

No one asks you to go for a beer at 6am or 7am, therefore getting your gym work or some light exercise done at this time means it is done and out of the way. Should you get invited out socially in the evening, you can attend, safe in the knowledge you have already done some exercise that day.

In Your Success Podcast episode 19, property investor and professional speaker Jackie Tomes explained the importance of habits and routines:

"Get routines and habits in place to make sure that you're consistently moving things forward. It is very easy to spend your life being a busy fool, just focusing on the urgent stuff and not actually prioritizing the time to do the important stuff, which is generally the goal setting and the strategy time. I'm a big fan of time blocking. For example, I use an online calendar and I literally block out the whole of the year and put in recurring reminders about where I'm spending time, basically moving my goals forward, moving my business forward from a bigger picture strategic point of view."

Plan your days, plan your meals, plan when you are going to go to the gym, to avoid not having any options when time is more limited. The path to great success happens one day at a time, and small changes to your habits will compound into big changes in your life.

Summary

- An ability to control your response to the external environment is one of the most important traits of success.
- Within environment, the people you associate with will have the greatest impact on your future potential – you can often predict where someone will be in five years by looking at their immediate circle. Avoid crab mentality and surround yourself with people who want you to win.
- To enhance your environment, audit who you spend the most time with, where you spend your time, what you spend your time doing, and what you consume in both your mind and mouth.
- Whilst it is tempting to build everything by yourself, you will achieve a lot more and go further with a team of great people surrounding you. Imagine a team of talented people all working towards your singular vision, people who will both inspire and challenge you along the way.
- Consider outsourcing some low-value tasks or responsibilities that you do not enjoy as a low-cost way of freeing up your time to spend on building your vision and implementing your success plan.
- Habits and paradigms control your day to day life, often without you being consciously aware of them. Take control of these to master any negative or bad habits or to reconstruct any paradigms that do not positively serve you.

Action Steps

1. Write down five positive things about your current environment (including the positive people you associate with).
2. Write down five things in your environment that you would like to change (including people that you perhaps could spend less time with).
3. Complete the Chapter 7 tasks in the Your Success Toolkit (available at www.yoursuccesspodcast.com/toolkit) including practical ways to enhance your environment and improve your habits.

Chapter 8

Communication

SUCCESS TRAIT 8:
Successful people are effective communicators, both internally and externally

Possessing good communication skills is a not a given. Sure, we can all talk, but can you effectively communicate your message in words, tonality, and body language? In this chapter, the art of communication will be examined, how to create a great first impression, and insight into how you can help influence and leverage the power of networks. Whole books have been written on the art of communication – we have put together the key points you need to be aware of, so that you can improve your chances of being noticed and listened to in a positive way.

Did you know that it takes an average of seven seconds to make an impression? Once that impression is made, it takes a long time to overwrite it. So, you need to get it right the first time and quickly.

You will learn how your words, tonality and body language, combined in the right way, will help you to successfully influence, negotiate or instruct, as required.

Your success is directly correlated with your ability to communicate: both with others and with yourself (your internal dialogue).

Talking to Yourself and the Law of Attraction

You are what you say. The language you use determines both your internal and external perception. Do you use the word 'depressed' a lot? Do you use the word 'bored' a lot? Are there a lot of negative words that you say throughout the day? Maybe it is time to address this, as whether you realise it or not, you are what you say, and others respond to the language you use; perhaps replace those words with more positive words.

You attract what you give out. If you are constantly negative, then you are probably going to receive negative things. If you have a positive outlook on life, then people will naturally want to spend time with you. The same is true of your vision. Your success could very well depend on attracting the right kind of people to work with you to help you achieve it. If they trust and like you and your vision is aligned to theirs, then you will have potentially found a great partner.

Are you seeking people who you could partner up with to accelerate your success plan? Are you saying or putting out the right energy for people to want to connect with you? The law of attraction is very powerful, and as such you should always be mindful of what you say and how you present yourself to others. What you give out is what you get back!

Try it for yourself. If someone asks you about the progress of your plan for your success and you reply with:

"It's going OK, I can't complain. There have been some problems lately but I'm still going," what kind of message does that communicate to the other person, and yourself?

Now consider the reaction you think you will get if you reply to the same question with the following:

"Things are going really well. I am so glad I am working on my passion. I had a problem the other day and although it was a difficult problem to solve, I have learnt so much from it." Who are they more likely to want to continue the conversation with?

Successful entrepreneurs seldom complain when faced with a negative situation. They try and look for the opportunity in every negative situation they encounter. Should everything fail in their business, they will see it as a great learning opportunity, a hard lesson, but a learning opportunity nevertheless. They will probably start all over again, this time armed with the knowledge and experience of why it failed in the first place and avoid the same mistakes again.

'Open' Versus 'Closed' Questions

An open-ended question will result in a detailed reply from the person answering it and a closed question will result in a short answer – usually either a 'yes' or 'no'. This is a common technique used by TV and radio interviewers to get more out of their interviewees.

Spot the difference between these two sentences.

1. Did you enjoy working on the film?
2. What was your favourite thing about working on the film?

There is a time and place for open and closed questions. A Police Officer might want to get to the bottom of the situation quickly and use straight to the point questions to ascertain what to do next.

A good manager could want to go through the decision-making process used by someone new in a job who had made a small mistake, to understand how they arrived at that decision, and will therefore want to use open-ended questions.

A practical application of this, both internally when talking to yourself and externally when talking to others, would be using open-ended questions to solve problems. For example, how can we solve this problem? What can we do to achieve a specific goal?

In a conversation, make sure you allow time for the other person to speak or think, and allow them to finish making their point before you jump in with a response. The art of conversation is more about listening than it is about speaking. Most people listen with the intent of responding rather than with the intent of understanding.

As the adage goes, we were given two ears and one mouth for a reason!

Ego and Empathy

Ego: such a small word, and yet it has caused countless arguments and conflict throughout history. One person's ego vs another's ego – oh, many pointless arguments have happened when neither side will back down or compromise. How many souls have been sacrificed to appease one leader's ego against another's? As Val McKie, author of Heartset, said, "WAR is an acronym for We Are Right."

We all have an ego (unless you're a Vulcan like Spock of Star Trek) and keeping control of your emotions can help you in many situations. You are less likely to argue unnecessarily with people and you are more likely to negotiate and get better terms if you remove the ego from matters. Plus, you are more likely to read other people better and have a clearer understanding of what is going on compared to others who might lose perspective or their composure should they lose control of their emotions. Do not let the 'red mist' of anger descend over your decision-making abilities. Rarely are well thought-out decisions made in a state of rage.

Empathy is the number-one skill required when communicating with other people. Listening to other people, understanding their point of view, and then expressing your own thoughts, wishes, feelings, and requirements in words and ways that the other person understands is amazingly powerful. You will find that your power of influence will increase greatly if you can achieve this skill.

We, often unknowingly, project our own beliefs on to other people and believe they think the same way as we do or will respond in a similar manner to how we would respond. However, if we are empathetic towards the other person, we will understand their point of view and we will be better placed to understand how they may react to something.

In Dale Carnegie's book 'How to Win Friends and Influence People' there is a chapter entitled 'You Can't Win an Argument', in which Carnegie writes that it is impossible to win an argument, because if lose it, you lose it, and if you win it, it's actually more of a loss because the other person goes away from the argument resenting you and either still firmly believing they were right, or embarrassed that you have called them out, potentially in public.

Having a greater understanding of someone else's point of view will greatly improve both your appreciation of other people's viewpoints and also help you negotiate better when required.

You Are Unique, so Be Your Authentic Self

People buy people. There are some schools of thought that say you have to fake it till you make it. What is an investor, business partner, or a customer likely to believe: someone who is being genuine or someone who is putting on a show and acting like who they think they should be?

Even if you do manage to pull off a convincing act in front of the person you are trying to impress, how long do you think you can keep the facade going for? Inevitably the real you will shine through. Remember that trust is earned and should be treated like a flat, smooth piece of paper. As soon as the trust is broken, it will be very difficult to re-establish. Think of that flat, smooth piece of paper. If you scrunch it up (trust broken) and try and make it smooth again (re-establish trust), it will never be truly smooth again. That is how you should treat your relationship with everyone; just be yourself. You are unique, so why not be who you are? You will never please everyone so there is no point even trying.

If you believe that you have the ability but perhaps you are at an early stage of your journey, it is acceptable to project an image of what you are hoping the end result will look like, as long as you feel you are remaining true to your core values. This comes down to the intent. If you are intending to deceive someone, that is wrong, but if you are intending to serve them, that is OK.

Be the person that you want to become; display the traits, professionalism, time keeping, and knowledge that would be expected. Just because you haven't done it before, doesn't mean that you can't start now. This is not about 'fake it until you make it' - it's all about the intention – do you intend to serve or deceive the other person?

Building and Communicating Your Brand

Steve Jobs, via his company Apple Inc., built a brand that will stand the test of time. Yes, he achieved an incredible amount during his lifetime, but his lasting legacy exists because he did a shameless amount of self-promotion alongside creating revolutionary products.

Building a brand is important because you want to stand out from the crowd, and not just be lost in the noise of all the other people wanting to be noticed. By building a good brand, you become recognisable and the law of attraction will start working in your favour.

Becoming the voice of authority in your specialism will position you as a go-to expert. This will start to pique interest and lead other people to refer to you as someone who will probably be able to answer their questions, or take some kind of action because of your unique contacts.

Taking this further, should someone bring a problem to the network and you can solve it, there could be an opportunity for you to be the group's expert or trouble-shooter. This could lead to chances for you to be paid for your time and expertise. Because you stuck your head above the parapet you could be rewarded with opportunities.

Should your success plan involve becoming a public figure, there could be some lucrative sponsorship opportunities for you. Should an established brand align their values with yours, then their marketing department could see a partnership with you as being beneficial to both sides and again, there are opportunities to be rewarded handsomely.

Become an influencer in your field to really make a difference and implement real change for the betterment of society. Adding value to society is key.

For example, within politics, you could become an influencer if you are noticed and trusted by the voting public. You want people to remember who you are quickly and for the right reasons. Perhaps you do not agree with certain companies in a particular field and how they are reacting to world events, or you can see a better way of serving the public. If this is the case, then why not do something positive that makes a difference in people's lives by being the change that people want?

Building Networks

The size of your net worth is directly related to the size of your network!

Your network is the group of people that you connect with on a regular or semi-regular basis. It could be a local network meeting you attend, it could be your immediate circle of friends and family, it could be your work colleagues, or it could be part of a mastermind group. How big is your network?

Why Is Your Net Worth Related to the Size of Your Network?

By having a large pool of people whom you have a connection with, you can tap into the power of that network. Here are some examples of the power of a network:

- Have you ever had a question that a search engine couldn't answer? You can put the question out to the network and you will hopefully get a wide-ranging set of answers for you to select from.
- Have you ever wanted to borrow money, but not from a bank? Who in your network do you know who has money that they might consider lending to you for a good return? Then, how you position yourself within that network could be key to gaining people's trust so that they want to work with you.
- Do you have a book that you are writing and would like some feedback on the cover design or even need some peer reviews? Put it out to the network and get some feedback.
- Do you have a question about how to build a boat? Join a group of boat-building specialists and you will no doubt have access to a whole plethora of expertise!

Networks offer a whole wealth of knowledge and experience that you alone could not possibly hope to have immediately. By establishing and making use of your network, you are leveraging other people's expertise and experience to help you.

Of course, it is a two-way street. If others in the network require help, then of course, try and help others in the network as much as possible. The law of reciprocity very much applies here and do not forget that you yourself will also be considered to be part of someone else's network.

Perfecting Your 30-Second Elevator Pitch

Bearing in mind that most people will have formed an opinion about your character in the first 7 seconds, it is important to project an interesting and compelling image of yourself quickly and accurately. This is where creating a 30 second elevator pitch is essential.

So, what is a 30-second elevator pitch?

The pitch is a snapshot of who you are, what you do, and why it would be of benefit to the person to listen, it is as simple as that. It requires a lot of practice to make it sound natural and make it roll off your tongue easily.

Imagine the following scenarios:

You know someone whom you would like to impress with your business pitch and they are attending a networking meeting at the same time as you. You meet them, and they ask you what you do.

A. You stumble and say the following "err yeah, my name is Angelos and I do a bit of property and I run a podcast interviewing lots of people. It's pretty good and you should check it out."

or

B. You say with confidence "My name is Angelos Sanders and I am a property investor, helping investors make a better return on their money compared to just keeping their money in their bank account. I also host a great podcast called Your Success Podcast and it has inspired many people around the world. Would you like to know more?"

Which version of the pitch would you respond better to?

Let's create your pitch:

1. Who are you?
2. What do you do or are looking to do?
3. Why should the other person care?
4. What should the other person do? What action do you want them to take?

Now it is time to practise. Start by practising your pitch in private, in front of a mirror, so you can see what your facial expressions and body language look like as you deliver the pitch.

What is Your Body Doing?

Often the words being spoken do not match up with the person's body language and this undermines the spoken message. For example, say you wanted to convey a strong, powerful pitch to a potential investor and you say the words perfectly, but you have your hands in your pockets and avoid eye contact, then you will undermine all the good work your words are trying to achieve.

When you are practising your pitch in front of friends, or when you are talking with people, ask them to observe and give you feedback on the following:

- Your stance;
- The position of your feet;
- Eye contact with the other person;
- Whether you are standing tall or are slouched.

Are your hands often flapping around like the wind or tucked up safely in your pockets or are your arms crossed? The shy or inexperienced conversationalist, needs to ensure that their hands are under control and look like they are feeling completely relaxed, even if they are not feeling relaxed inside.

- Are your arms crossed?
- Are your hands fidgeting?
- Are your hands in your pocket?
- Are you touching your face nervously?

If being a confident conversationalist does not come naturally to you, then it will require lots of practice but like any skill, it is learnable. Think of a duck swimming on the surface of the water, perfectly calm and serene, and yet underneath the surface, it is paddling away vigorously and yet no one would know this if they were simply looking at the surface. The more practice and experience you have, the better your delivery will become and the clearer your message will be.

Once you have perfected your first pitch, why not create another for different scenarios, such as when you are at a different type of event. Perhaps this pitch could be deployed when you are making a first impression with a customer or a supplier at your work. For a more detailed analysis of pitches, and how to create your pitch, listen to Your Success Podcast, episode 14 and complete the action steps in the Your Success Toolkit.

Whilst it is essential that you have your 30-second elevator pitch practised, there may be situations where it is not appropriate to use a 30-second pitch, and a more conversational style is required. This is where creating a rapid rapport will help.

Rapid Rapport Creation

Have you ever wanted to make a great impression straight away?

Rapid rapport creation will allow you to feel comfortable in new social and formal environments and will accelerate your acceptance within new groups, making people feel more at ease with you. It will also be more fun for you as rapport is a two-way street.

Here are some tips on how to rapidly build a good connection with someone whom you might have just met for the first time.

- Keep the focus of the conversation on the other person. It's all about them. It's easy to talk about yourself as that is the subject we know the most about, but try to listen more during the conversation.
- Ask the other person about their hobbies and interests. Use what you already know about the person to bridge conversations to enquire deeper about that subject, or

about a different interest they have. Do they like cars or are they a big fan of a certain big band? Be genuinely interested in their responses; don't just pretend to be just to build rapport. People are quite astute when it comes to knowing if someone is being genuine or not.

- Enquire about and expand on things you have in common or mutual friends you have. Again, be genuinely interested.
- Be relaxed and laugh (genuinely) with the person over a situation. Perhaps you are both in a new environment and can share the oddness of the situation with each other.
- Ask questions and listen with the intent to understand; it's about them, not about you!

Although, on the face of it, some of tips might sound like 'tricks' or 'hacks', they are simply tools that allow us to fast track relationship building. You get to achieve the same outcome quicker and both parties feel a genuine connection with each other, much sooner in the relationship.

Rapid rapport creation is fundamental as the other person needs to like you and trust you before they will undertake any 'action' with you, be that a business transaction or an emotional relationship.

Summary

- Great communication, both internally and externally, is a key trait of success. This includes not only the words you use, but also your tonality and body language. It is important to use positive language instead of negative language as this can shape how both you and others react.
- Empathy is important when understanding other people's points of view and understanding how best to communicate with them.
- Become an influencer and build your brand, as this could open many doors, both in terms of your reach and who you can help, as well financial rewards.

- Present yourself in a confident manner and aim to establish rapport with the people you meet. Create a good and impactful 30-second elevator pitch to stand out from the crowd and also think about rapid rapport creation.
- To accelerate your success plan it is important to network far and wide, to ensure you spread the word of what you are looking for or how you can help others.
- Use rapid rapport creation to fast-track a genuine connection with another.

Action Steps

1. Try listening more than you talk and ask more open-ended questions in general conversation.
2. Tell everyone what you do or intend to do – you never know who is listening and can help you.
3. Complete the Chapter 8 tasks in the Your Success Toolkit (available at www.yoursuccesspodcast.com/toolkit) including creating and practising your 30 second elevator pitch.

Chapter 9

Action

SUCCESS TRAIT 9:
Successful people consistently take massive action

Taking action is one of the most important traits of success. Even if you know all of the theory, read all of the books, and have mentoring from the most successful people, none of this will mean anything unless you pull your finger out and get on with it!

It's all on you. No mentors, support groups, friends, family, or employers are going to help you along this journey unless you start to take action on living your dreams and working towards the success that you have defined for yourself in Chapter 1. If you put this book down now and take no action, your life will not change, and success will continue to be a distant dream.

But the good news is, you are in control! Yes, you! Sure, you can get support along the way, but you need to drive the actions that take you to the next level, in all areas of your life.

This chapter explores both the importance of taking massive action, as well as the need for consistency, how to stay focused, and avoid distractions on your path to success.

The Law of Attraction Is Not Enough

You may have heard before about 'putting your wishes out to the universe' or 'the law of attraction'. Whilst these may sound ethereal, they do work – but only if you follow up with massive action.

Putting what you want out to the universe is just the first step. It's an important step, as it's the realisation and communication of what you want, or what needs to happen in your life. But by far the most important part is taking the follow-up actions that start to build towards your vision of success.

Like a self-fulfilling prophecy, the more you talk about something with different people, the greater the chance is that it will happen. For example, if you keep saying how much you want tickets to a certain sold-out event, the more chance there is of someone saying "oh, I know someone who is selling their ticket".

Communicating what you want helps both cement in your own mind what you want to happen, as well as letting everyone know what path you are on; you will be surprised by who in your existing network of friends/family/work colleagues can help you on your journey. You just don't know who knows who until you start putting your dreams and desires out there.

Action Is Greater Than Talent

Whether due to natural-born talent or the conditions of their upbringing (see Chapter 7 – Environment for more on this), some people have a greater level of 'talent' in certain things, and as such may appear to find things easier to do.

But if that person does not take massive amounts of consistent action, they will be beaten by somebody less 'talented', but who has put in the work. The reason for this can be broken down in to two parts – **feedback** and **opportunity**:

1) Feedback: Those who take consistent amounts of massive action will have more experience and will likely 'fail' more often. However, with these experiences and failures, they are testing what works and what does not work, pushing the boundaries. Providing that they use this experience and feedback from the market, customers, and the universe, they will grow. With growth comes more success. The 'talented' person who rests on their laurels will not experience the growth or get the benefit of the feedback. These prodigies will soon be overtaken by the person who has less 'talent', but a greater work ethic.

2) Opportunity: Those who take consistent amounts of massive action will be luckier. As the famous adage goes, "the harder I work, the luckier I get". Those who 'do' more get presented with more opportunities. That could be becoming known in a particular niche as the go-to person, or doors opening up for you as you network and make more connections that then open you up to their network. In terms of opportunity, there is also 'being in the right place at the right time'. Those who take consistent amounts of massive

action find themselves in the right place, at the right time, far more often. It's indisputable that if you are in more places (that are aligned to your overall vision for success), taking more action (again, action aligned to your vision), you will be presented with more opportunity which can aide you in your path towards your vision. As is sometimes said, luck is when preparation meets opportunity.

It is important not to underestimate the amount of action you will need to take towards your vision of success. Everything takes more work than you realise, and there will be more challenges than you think there will be.

How can you possibly estimate the amount of time and effort required to do something you've never done? Therefore, if you think you need to make ten sales calls to get a single sale, you probably need to make 100. If you think you need to view five properties before you find the one you want to put an offer on, you probably need to view 50. If you think it will take a year to get to financial 'freedom', it will probably take two, or three, or five. But do not let this put you off, as the rewards when you reach your vision of success will be worth it. This is exactly why you need to be committed, not just interested.

Are You Committed, or Just Interested?

There is a big difference between being *interested* in something and being 100% *committed* to it. If you are merely interested in something, you will get distracted, you will delay it, and you will re-prioritise other tasks above it. Eventually you will give up, usually justifying it to yourself along the way with various excuses.

Being absolutely committed to achieving an outcome is what is required to actually achieve it. This is why your goals and milestones need to be aligned to your vision of success; if you are truly going to commit to something, you had better be sure that it is actually what you want. This is because when you commit to it, it will happen.

Being committed to an outcome means it takes precedence. Being committed to losing weight or adding lean muscle mass means ordering salad and not drinking alcohol when everyone else at the table is having the steak and chips with a large glass of wine.

Being committed to passing an exam means studying that extra hour and not watching your favourite TV programme, the one that all of your friends and family are talking about.

Being committed to saving money (in order to invest) means getting the bus instead of the taxi, it means making a packed lunch and taking it in to work, and it means not going on holiday – even if everyone you know is going away for the summer.

Being committed is doing what is right, not what is easy, which is why it is so important that what you commit to is what you truly want.

As Alexander the Great showed, it adds real steel to your resolve if you burn your boats so there is no plan B. This means, you must not give yourself an opportunity to slip back in to mediocrity. Now, this doesn't mean that you should burn down all of your bridges and relationships. For example, if you quit your job to pursue your passion, make sure you leave on good terms with your employer.

Whilst you don't want to give yourself the easy option of going back to work if self-employed life doesn't work out for you, if you are staying in the same industry your previous employer might still be a useful contact to have or even be a future client of yours!

In addition to this, people will judge you on your interactions with others and decide if they want to work with you. So, whilst you may not care what your now ex-boss thinks of you, an outburst may have a lasting impact on your reputation.

Here are some examples of how you can take action today to set yourself up to win:

- Pack your gym bag before you go to bed, so you can just pick it up in the morning.
- Sell your TV (or at least put it into storage) if you are committed to not watching TV until you have written that new business plan.
- Prepare the next day's lunch before you go to bed and leave a post-it note by the door to remind you. Don't take any cash to ensure you save money on lunches and eat healthily.
- Make it financial: there is nothing like putting some money on the line as motivation. As discussed in Chapter 2 – Motivation and Inspiration, inspiration can be a short-term thing, but that doesn't mean it can't be used to help fully commit to achieving an outcome.
- Tell everyone you know about something you want to achieve so it becomes too embarrassing to even come close to failing, plus you will also get the additional benefit of receiving support.

We believe you can do it too. You have invested time and money reading this book and completing the tasks in the Your Success Toolkit – therefore, you have a curiosity – a spark of ambition – to make a change in your life.

Whilst it is imperative that you are absolutely committed, you also need to remain focused.

Focus

Progress towards success is impaired by constantly switching from one idea, business or job to another. At best this will severely delay you, at worst it will cause your success plan to fail completely, result in a lack of confidence and introduce doubt that you will ever achieve what you desire.

FOCUS is often referred to as standing for '**F**ollow **O**ne **C**ourse **U**ntil **S**uccessful', which is a useful way to think about working solely on the main priorities that align with your vision of success, and ignoring everything else.

Distractions, often called 'shiny pennies', will be plentiful. You need to be able to navigate around these.

'Shiny penny syndrome' is a phrase that means stopping, changing course, restarting, exploring new opportunities, and stopping what you're already doing to start something new. This will divert you away from the course that you were travelling on, the progress that you've made, and the concentration and momentum that you had built up.

Think of seeing a shiny penny on the floor, stopping what you are doing, and picking it up.

The cautionary tale of 'shiny penny syndrome' is that constantly stopping, starting and changing course can mean that success, whatever that means in terms of results – financial, health-wise, familial – actually never ends up happening as not enough time and energy is committed to making the one thing happen, before jumping to the next thing. The compound effect is not being allowed to work its magic.

The Compound Effect

Author and personal development expert Darren Hardy explained that the compound effect is the act of repeatedly doing something day in and day out until it becomes a habit – it becomes part of your psyche. Although you may not necessarily see the results straight away, you compound it over four to five weeks, a month to two months, or over a year, and before you know it you have achieved significant progress towards your goal and those habits have become ingrained within you.

Probably the easiest example everyone can relate to is the art of walking when you were a baby or toddler. When you first stand up on your legs as a baby, and you fall down, you don't think to yourself "oh forget this walking business, it's not for me!", and your parents certainly don't think "oh yeah it's not for them; they're not going to be a walker!"

You keep going, minute after minute, hour after hour, with multiple failures behind you, you slowly are able to walk. That's the compound effect in action.

From a business point of view, here is a very simplified example:

- You start a business and you have zero customers on day one.
- No one knows about you, but you manage to get one customer. You give them a great experience. You have one product, one customer. They love it.
- They go home and they tell two people. Maybe one of those people decides to become a customer then you have two customers. So, you are starting to build some momentum.
- Then you do some marketing. You may attract five more customers and you treat those five customers the same (you give them a great experience). They go off and they tell people, friends and family.
- You rinse and repeat that, you add in free and paid marketing, and you bring in referrals. You eventually sell to a thousand customers.

When you are ready to launch a new product, you're in a great position, given that you've got a thousand customers who know you, who like you and have bought from you. You have obviously delivered excellent customer service and products; do you think it would take another year for you to sell to another thousand customers?

It probably wouldn't. It might depend on what the product is, but it would probably not take as long as your initial launch because you already have that momentum, you already have some brand awareness, you already have customers, and you've also had feedback on what type of marketing works for your business.

You have also tested your profit margins and profitability. If you had stopped, say, halfway through, and you'd gone off to do something different, you would never have built that momentum, built that customer base, and gained that feedback with trust.

This concept is also referred to as 'the dip', popularised by Seth Godin's book of the same name. The dip is about the outpouring of money and time, resources and effort, before you see any tangible results. It's all up-front work (meaning the work is at the beginning with little or no pay-off, with the major pay-out towards the end). You go through the dip in income and the dip in the amount of money you put into it, but there's no immediate payback.

If you keep stopping, starting, and changing direction, you will move from one dip to another and never actually get out of any of the dips.

A Penny Every Day Vs One Million Dollars

This explains the compound effect beautifully. Imagine being given a once in a lifetime choice between two ways of getting rich.

Option 1: You are offered a penny that doubles every day for 30 days. So, one penny becomes two pence on day two, becomes four pence, on day three, and so on.

Option 2: You are offered a lump sum of £1,000,000 on day one.

Which option would you accept?

If you accepted Option 2, then that would be a good and safe option: you have the lump sum straight away and off you go to enjoy your £1,000,000!

Now let's look at Option 1.

There are no investments that we know of that double every day (please write in if you encounter any on your travels!) but the point here is if you picked Option 1, then for the first 10 days you have made just £5.12. That's nothing, right?

Another seven days pass, and you have made a mere £655. At this point you might be tempted to throw in the towel thinking you will never become a millionaire at this rate!

Hold on, as this is where things are about to get interesting.

As we hit days 18-21, we rocket up from £1,310 to £5,242 – now things are happening! For the last nine days there is phenomenal growth. The point is that only in the last few days of the 30-day journey, do we see great results. If you had given up before then, you never would have realised your full potential.

By day 30, the one penny has become a massive £5,338,709!

This proves that slow, steady consistency can be extremely powerful, even if in the early days it looks like it may be 'underperforming' – all it needs is time.

The Concept of the 20-Mile March

Jim Collins and Morten T. Hansen popularised the term '20-Mile March' to refer to a consistent amount of effort applied to a task over a period of time, rather than a fluctuation between high intensity activity and low intensity activity. The theory is that, if you walked 20 miles per day over a sustained period of time, this would be better than walking 40-50 miles in good weather conditions and then much less or not at all when the weather was less pleasant.

Collins and Hansen discovered the story of adventurers Robert Falcon Scott and Roald Amundsen, and their race to reach the South Pole, and drew parallels between the story of the explorers and the 20-Mile March theory.

Amundsen beat Scott to the South Pole in 1911 and made it back safely with his team. Scott reached the South Pole in second place, but he and his men died. Among other factors that contributed to the contrasting successes of these two men, Collins and Hansen found that Amundsen carried out the expedition with 'methodical, disciplined consistency' and stuck to the plan he had created.

You can apply some of the key components of the 20-Mile March to your success journey:

- **Tailor your vision** – ensure your vision is what you truly want and not defined by anyone else.
- **Set clear Key Performance Indicators (KPIs)** – set your vision and your goals and track your progress against these.
- **Impose Constraints** – focus on only what is important in pursuit of your vision.
- **Have the ability to control** – ensure that your vision and

goals are largely within your own control to achieve.

- **Be SMART** – set SMART targets and measure progress against these.
- **Be consistent** – as this chapter states, consistently take massive action.

Avoid Distractions

We are constantly bombarded by distractions. Emails, text alerts, phone calls and social media notifications are all constantly vying for our attention. Unfortunately, people have been conditioned to respond immediately to this barrage of distraction.

Whilst you may well use these tools for work purposes or to pursue your vision, for the most part these will distract you from what you actually need to be doing and spending time on. Perhaps you could switch the distractions off when you need to do any kind of focused work. Maybe a complete cut-off is difficult for you, then you can always chunk your time out, where you schedule your break time during the day so that you are more disciplined when replying to the world's wants. Remember, if you are not working on achieving your success by focusing on implementing your plan, you are helping others achieve their vision by constantly replying and being distracted.

The lost momentum and energy in stopping what you are doing to read an email or go on social media is incredible. Whilst you may think that taking a five-minute break to check up on what's going on in the world is only going to delay you by five minutes, in actual fact, restarting what you were previously doing (if it had any kind of thinking attached to it) will take anywhere from 10 minutes to 30 minutes. Or, you may not be able to get back into 'flow' and you may have to defer the activity to another day!

The Pomodoro Technique is a time management concept that Francesco Cirillo developed in the 1980s. This involves breaking work down into chunks (or 'Pomodoros') which traditionally were 25 minutes in length, separated by a short break of three to five minutes. After four Pomodoros, you would take a longer break of 15-30 minutes.

This (or something similar that works for you), is a great way to retain focus, but still allow time for breaks which are an important part of any activity that requires any kind of mental or physical energy.

In addition, the planning and preparation that goes into actually working out what you have to do, how long it will take, and putting this into the Pomodoro framework is a key part of the technique.

Whilst avoiding distractions is key, sometimes you just need to say 'no'.

The Ability to Say 'No'

Richard Branson is regularly quoted as having said, "If someone offers you an opportunity and you're not sure if you can do it, say yes and figure out how to do it later."

This is a great life philosophy for overcoming limiting beliefs and not getting overwhelmed by the detail of how to achieve something. However, he did not mean that you should say 'yes' to **everything**.

The sentiment is to not be afraid if you can't do something right now, as you have time to figure it out and work out how you'll be able to do it. Don't write yourself off up-front because you don't know if you can do it until you have tried it!

However, new opportunities take resources (time, money, mental capacity), so when a new idea or concept is presented to you, you need to really assess both whether it is supporting your vision and getting you closer to it and also what impact will taking on the new opportunity have. For example, taking a new job that means working longer hours may mean you have more cash in the short term, but may result in having less time to work on your passion and build a business or career that you love: your long-term goal. This isn't always the case, but it's important to be honest with yourself about the impact when considering new business and personal opportunities in life.

Do not limit yourself by saying "I can't do that as I don't have the skills", but at the same time, be honest about the time and money commitment that new opportunities will have on your life and your current success journey.

The ability to stay focused and say 'no' to opportunities that do not serve your vision will be a determining factor in your success journey.

Get Perfect Later

Starting now is better than doing nothing and waiting for the perfect time or set of circumstances (which rarely come by the way). However, this doesn't mean throwing all caution to the wind and not thinking realistically about the future.

If you want to quit your job and pursue a self-employed career, don't just hand in your notice and shout "it's okay, I'm starting now, and I'll get perfect later". It's sensible to think practically about how you will receive an income, how much you need, and how long it will take to set up a new business. Don't let this paralyse you into inaction, waiting for the stars to align and the perfect set of circumstances before you make that leap. Formulate a plan, account for all of the known potential risks, ask for advice where you need to, and then just do it!

As successful, but (self-styled) 'lazy' entrepreneur John Lamerton stated in Your Success Podcast episode 38:

"The perfectly worded sales letter that never gets sent will always be beaten by the crap version that actually just goes out. Screw it. Send it out."

If you have a great idea and believe it could really do well, getting it out there to the market and being first is very important.

It is better to have something rough and ready for consumers to buy and give you feedback on rather than to wait for the best time when everything is perfected. Because you are first to market, you are also earning something from the product: feedback. With feedback from customers, you are then able to release version two where you have ironed out any problems with the product. The key is that you released it out there initially.

Writing a book is a good example of this concept. An author might keep revisiting their drafts and editing every line again and again, and yet not adding anything of value. Just get it published and let the public decide on what works and what could be improved. There is always a second edition to make adjustments and amendments.

The best definition of an entrepreneur is: jumping out of a plane and building your parachute on the way down.

Avoiding Overwhelming Circumstances

If you find yourself not taking action or making a change in a certain area of your life, it may be because you are feeling overwhelmed by a goal or milestone.

If this is the case, it will help you to break the overall goal or milestone down in to manageable tasks that you can start to act on straight away. Below is an example of where a large goal is broken down into more easily achievable chunks.

How do you get a new job? It seems like an extremely daunting and overwhelming task, something which is so big in scale that it prevents some people taking the necessary action. However, it can be broken down into a set of simple actions that follow on from each other:

1. Research job vacancies.
    a. Where are job vacancies likely to be advertised?
    b. What salary are you looking for?

c. Will you outsource it and ask a recruitment agent to find a job opening for you?

d. Do you need to re-train or update your skillset?

2. Speak to people doing the job now.

   a. Speak with people who have experience in the job to find out what you are getting yourself into. This could open your eyes to the reality of the situation and help inform your decision-making process.

3. Write CV and covering letter.

   a. You need to dust off your old CV and update it with all the new skills you have acquired in your existing job.

   b. Have it peer-reviewed by friends, family, or experts, so it looks great.

   c. Customise it so it applies to the new company you are applying to.

4. Apply for jobs.

   a. Your CV is polished, you have sent it out to lots of potential employers, and you are feeling confident.

   b. You email, you make phone calls and you follow up with a written letter.

5. Attend interview.

   a. You have managed to get your foot through the door, which is always the hardest part. Now is the time to really impress.

   b. You will be asked a barrage of questions and first impressions really count – see Chapter 8 on Communication and how to make a great first impression quickly. If you want to know what goes through the interviewer's mind, then have a listen to Your Success Podcast episode 48 to help you see it from the other side of the table.

6. Get job offer letter.

   a. You open the email or letter or take the call with trepidation. It's good news! Great job! All that hard work has paid off, you tell your friends and family, and all is well with the world for a short while.

7. Write resignation letter.
   a. You write your resignation letter and give it to your current boss.
8. Start new job.
   a. This is it – the big day! New faces, new roles, new office, new opportunities, and a renewed sense of enthusiasm.

There is a certain amount of irony among people looking for a new job who want nothing more than getting the job they desire. Yet, fast forward a few months and they are still in the same situation: that Sunday evening dread of going to work kicks in and they begin to resent their situation all over again. How many smiling faces do you see on your way to work on a Monday morning?

As you can appreciate, changing jobs is usually not an easy process. Just like changing your job, planning and achieving your success will seem like a large, daunting goal. To achieve it, you need to break it down into manageable chunks.

Sometimes you will believe that everything is on track and then you will be knocked back, but you will continue as you know how important achieving your success is. Having perseverance was discussed in more detail in Chapter 4.

You will also see that chunking large goals into smaller targets will give you multiple small successes along the way. This will give you more wins and boost your productivity and spirits more often.

Similar to how money makes more money, when you start becoming successful, people will take notice. Some might ask you how you are doing it, thus indirectly enquiring as to how they can achieve their own success.

Summary

- There are no two ways about it: you must take action to achieve your success plan. Are you committed or just interested?
- It is important to start now and get perfect later as you will get valuable feedback on what can be improved once you have started. Push those boundaries of success!
- Action is greater than talent when talent doesn't work hard enough.
- Your ability to say 'no' will be imperative to your success. Although it will be hard passing on certain opportunities, it will be worth it. Focus is key to success – do not be distracted by shiny pennies.
- To avoid overwhelm, break large milestones down in to smaller tasks that you can action right away and start to experience progress immediately; this will spur you on to do more

Action Steps

1. What could you start doing now? Write down some ideas that you might be procrastinating over starting; perhaps you're waiting for the perfect time to start. The time is now!
2. Write down some examples of the 'shiny pennies' you have encountered over the past couple of years, and list whether they are aligned with your vision, or whether they distract you from your main activity which is leading towards your vision of success.
3. Complete the Chapter 9 tasks in the Your Success Toolkit (available at www.yoursuccesspodcast.com/toolkit) including ways to say 'no' to opportunities that are not aligned with your vision, but leave the door open for future conversations.

Chapter 10

Long-Term Success

SUCCESS TRAIT 10:
Successful people maintain their traits consistently, for long term success

As discussed throughout this book, success is a journey as opposed to a destination. A lot of people never feel like they have 'made it'. This is primarily because the very nature of ambition is that it reaches for higher levels as success is achieved. This is why you often hear the term 'levelling up' to describe an activity or skill that was previously outside of your comfort zone or ability level at a previous point in time.

Once you have achieved what you once perceived to be an ambitious goal, it is unlikely that you will stop.

Sure, you might reach a certain business goal, family goal, or sum of money that you had in mind, but, the reality is that as soon as that goal is reached (or even before), the target will shift, either to a larger business, impact, financial goal, or to something totally different. Did you ever wish for a car and that was all you ever wanted, but as soon as you had the car, you spotted them everywhere on the road and then started thinking about the next one?

This chapter is all about maintaining success for the long term by consistently upholding the traits of success that helped you get there in the first place. There's no such thing as a destination for success – your ambition expands as you grow. So, when you refer to having 'achieved' your success in this chapter, this will be referring to achieving a certain level of success that you define, not necessarily being the end goal where you would stop growing.

It is important to ensure you do not become complacent when things start to turn around in your life. Preserving your deserved success to see you through your life and leaving something amazing for your family and for the broader society is an inspiring goal to strive for.

Levels of Success

As soon as you have reached any level of success (or more than likely before you have gotten there, but once you know you are on your way), your goals and ambitions will have grown.

A very simple example that shows this is earning money. It may be inconceivable to a student earning minimum wage working in a bar that they could ever get paid more than about £20,000 per year. Once they reach this figure for earnings and have built their confidence, skillset, and understanding of the world, they might target £30,000 per year. Surely that is the most anyone would ever be prepared to pay them. But once they earn that and can see real-life reference points for people earning £40,000 per year, this then becomes the new target and expectation for their new norm.

In each case, the opportunity existed in the world for that person to earn £40,000 (or more), but what held them back was:

1. Their belief about of their own self-worth,

and

2. The skillset required to actually be proficient in the job that pays £40,000.

If we think of this as levels – with level 1 representing £10,000 per year and level 10 representing £100,000 per year – there is nothing stopping someone at level one applying for a job with a level 10 salary, provided that they can evidence the skillset to complete this job and have the relevant experience. More likely, people move up the levels one or two at a time, growing each time as a person. At the same time, they are broadening both their own perceived self-worth and also the demonstrable competency to deliver at that new level.

This is why people rarely get to a point where they say they are 'successful' or they have achieved everything they wanted, and similar to a personal trainer telling you to complete 20 push ups and once you have completed 20, saying do another 10, then you achieve another 10. The goalposts are constantly changing. This is far from being a bad thing; in fact, it is essential for the continued evolution and development of the human race.

It is because of the ever-growing and broadening nature of goals, targets and success, that it is important to have perspective and gratitude for what you have achieved before moving to the next level.

Perspective and Gratitude

Perspective and gratitude were discussed in Chapter 4 – Determination and Perseverance, but it is worth adding the following: gratitude is not just about being grateful for what you have when you first start goal setting, you need to maintain it as you grow and achieve more success, and in fact it becomes even more important.

The ability to look back at where you have come from and be grateful for the opportunities you have had will become more and more important as you set bigger and more audacious goals for yourself. As you grow, and as these goals become bigger, the potential to fail still exists – either more often or on a larger scale. During this time, it's important to not lose perspective on both how far you have come, how well you have done, and what you have – especially compared to people who are further behind in their success journey than you are.

Yes, if a business deal goes wrong and you lose the opportunity to make some serious money, or you don't get that acting role you really wanted, it will hurt. However, the ability to be grateful that you were even in a position to do big deals, or that you even had the audition for the role in the first place, will keep you grounded and prevent the feeling of constantly being unfulfilled as you stretch outside of your comfort zone and create new opportunities.

When you face adversity, particularly when you are more advanced in your success journey, think back to five, ten, or fifteen years ago when you were first starting out. How grateful would your younger self be for the opportunities you have now? They would have zero expectation of anything coming from it.

If you retain a sense of this and balance it with the drive and ambition that got you to where you are now, you will be a truly unstoppable force!

Time to Reflect

Take time to reflect on your journey to-date. You have no doubt put in countless hours of hard work and effort and ignored lots of tempting distractions in order to achieve your success.

You have worked incredibly hard to reach this point, but sometimes hitting your goal can be both mentally and physically exhausting. Do you need a break? If you do, take it and allow yourself some down time, free from work. Allow yourself to enjoy a couple of weeks on the beach or go on a driving weekend with an awesome sports car. Do whatever floats your boat and most importantly, don't feel guilty about taking time out to enjoy yourself – you deserve it!

When you have worked so long on creating your success, having started from scratch and completing this phase of it, and having felt long periods of uncertainty, it can sometimes be hard to let go and allow yourself to relax. But you must recharge.

Even if you did not really believe when you started your journey, you cracked on anyway and you actually achieved your success, well done you! It can take some time for us to accept that we have actually made it. Take a moment to reflect, be grateful for what you have achieved. We have already said that success is a journey and not a destination, there are key milestones that you will have hit and perhaps they are significant milestones which have taken a lot of blood, sweat, and tears along the way. Sometimes the sense of disbelief can wash over you when you actually make it! Therefore, it is very important for you not to only enjoy the moment, but to accept it as well.

Accept that you have achieved something unique and hard fought for, something that few people have managed to achieve in their own lives. Do yourself a favour and take some time out for yourself and enjoy it. This will help you both now and also when moving forward to the next milestone. Time off will recharge you and also give you a mental boost you need as you have trained your brain to realise there is a reward once you have reached a significant milestone.

Retire or Reload?

'Retirement'. Depending on your age, this word might have different meanings for you. An older person might think, after completing their success journey that now would be a good time to retire, relax, and enjoy the finer things in life. A younger person might like the idea of retirement, however, winding down when you are at the peak of your life might not be the best thing to do as there is so much left to give.

There are lots of cases where people have spent a lifetime working in a company, and upon retiring they age rapidly as they have lost the routine that they have been used to for many decades. Suddenly, they feel adrift with nothing to wake up for as all they have ever known was the work environment.

This is why you must have something to keep you occupied when you stop work to either retire or when you have completed your success plan. What hobby have you put on the back burner for many years that you now have the time to actually learn about and do? Maybe there is a sport you have fancied trying or maybe cruising around the world with your loved one is what you have always dreamed about.

Perhaps retirement is not for you now and maybe you are not happy with the status quo; let's not forget that we as humans are ideally suited to constant growth, both mentally and physically.

Perhaps a new challenge is what you need and yearn for. You are becoming addicted to the rush of achieving new things, while pushing yourself well and truly outside of your comfort zone. Could you outdo your achievement and take it to another level?

Is there another gift or talent you have or possess to share with the world? Perhaps you should revisit earlier chapters on creating your new vision for your success.

Once you achieve your goal, unless you continuously re-plan your goals, you may experience a sense of emptiness within you and you could find yourself drifting without a new vision. Perhaps it is time to revisit your vision board. You can update it to reflect the new place that you are now at. Take it back to basics and set a new vision for yourself and family, or just build on what has come before.

Obsession vs Balance

This is the real test for your resolve and how much you really want to make your success journey a reality and change your life for the better.

You will have to be obsessed to make it happen. You will have to possess laser-like, single-minded focus. Perhaps this will be a new experience for you to both remain focused in the short-term and long-term.

It will be exhausting both physically and mentally, but mostly mentally as you will have not only the day to day running of your success journey but also keeping yourself and everything around you focused on achieving your vision.

This is where obsession comes into play. It will keep you pushing through, even when you are having down days. It will force you to get out of bed early when all you want to do is sleep. It will force you to work on strategy or doing admin when all you want to do is join your friends at the cinema.

You need to be obsessed in order to be successful – there is no secret formula to becoming a success. You also need bucket loads of hard work, determination, and a clear vision.

Are you prepared for such a commitment? Are your family and friends ready to support you on your journey? Will they offer you support when you feel those down days, even when they are sick and tired about hearing about your journey?

It is important to sit down with your family and friends to talk through with them why you are undertaking this journey, why it is so important to you and to ask for support. Let them know that you will need their support and understanding in the long term; if they are good friends, then they will understand and be patient with you. You might even inspire them to undertake their own success journey! Be aware that your newfound energy and impetus will be infectious!

A word of caution, though. Obsession is not usually a healthy thing for long periods of time without a couple of days off from your journey. Allow yourself a few days off just to unwind, recharge, and reflect on how things are progressing. Of course, you must have that absolute determination to achieve your success, but you must have balance in your life.

This is where balance comes into play. You do not want to be a blinkered horse which is running wild for miles on end but had lost its rider ages ago.

When to Let Go and Call It Quits

Pressing on for years in a failing business (or any venture) may not always be the smartest move, especially if you are losing money. Perhaps it is causing you unhappiness which in turn has a knock-on effect on your personal life.

So how do you know when to call it quits?

Really, the only answer here is that you have to be honest with yourself, as well as get advice from experienced people around you. Being told your business idea won't work and that you should quit by your mates down the pub is one thing that you can take with a pinch of salt. Being consistently rejected by customers, business partners, and those experienced in the industry you are in is possibly when you should start to doubt yourself.

Now, that's not to say that people who have been rejected hundreds or thousands of times haven't gone on to innovate and break the mould, but it's about being really honest with yourself and weighing peoples' advice according to their experience and vested interest in the outcome.

Ironically, human nature being what it is, there are some, who are stubborn and despite all the evidence are not willing give up and accept defeat. These people continue to plough on regardless. In these cases, the costs of victory in terms of time, effort, money, broken relationships etc. can be high and all to achieve a perceived victory at some point in the future. Is this type of victory really worth it?

Would You Like a Pyrrhic victory?

A great idiom which describes winning the battle but losing the war is the 'Pyrrhic Victory'.

Pyrrhus of Epirus (319/318 - 272BC) was an Ancient Greek King who was not happy with Ancient Rome's expansion into Greece. Pyrrhus fancied himself as a new Alexander the Great and set about halting and defeating the Romans. He won several battles against the Romans, but the losses to his own army were so great, it made him question whether to continue fighting the Romans or not.

Plutarch (Roman historian) quoted Pyrrhus as saying, "If we are victorious in one more battle with the Romans, we shall be utterly ruined!"

Eventually Pyrrhus realised there was no point 'winning' any more battles should his own army be destroyed in the process, so he retreated back to Greece.

He won many battles, but at what cost to himself? You might want something so badly and yet the personal cost to you is so significant that you must stop and ask yourself, "is victory really worth it?"

Do the rewards really outweigh all of the personal sacrifices you have endured along the way? The difficult part is taking a step back and looking at your situation in an objective manner. With the help of your team and trusted friends and family, you might be able to get another view on things. Hopefully, you are able to take their advice on board and make an informed decision.

Stay the course and put in the work to see if something will work for you. At the same time, don't let your ego take over and make you continue with something longer than you should, just to save face or try and prove to your friends and family that something will work.

It is a hard decision but it's just about being honest with yourself. Be honest with yourself regarding the things that you love to do, as well as the things that actually pay well, that you have experience in, that you can leverage, even if just for a short time.

Don't Get Complacent

Worst case scenario, even if you lost everything tomorrow, you could return to where you were again, as your experiences and what you have accomplished over the years could get you back to where you are now. What you have learnt, the connections you have made, the goodwill you have with people, and the relationships you have built can all still be maintained. You haven't invested in yourself and spent months, years, or even decades building something to then throw it away through becoming complacent.

Remember, stay true to the fundamentals that got you to where you are: your vision, your values, and your 'why'.

It is easy for complacency to set in when results start showing up, such as not making as many sales calls or following up as diligently, not treating customers number 987, 988 and 989 with the same level of care as you did with your first few customers. Perhaps you're not training as hard for a race, as you've been winning all the qualifying races, or not being as strict with your diet as you've already hit certain milestones.

The best way to continue on the same path, is to set new standards and have someone keep you accountable, well after results start showing up. So, keep your personal trainer, even after you've lost the weight. Instil your business's core values into your staff and use KPIs (key performance indicators) so they will maintain levels of customer service, long after you yourself have stopped performing customer-facing or operational roles.

Another way to ensure you do not get complacent comes back to environment: the focus of Chapter 7. If you constantly upgrade your environment and peer group to people with a greater vision and bigger goals, you will never become stale or get complacent. An athlete might start training with a local club, but if they are consistently winning races, they need to move up to competing at county level, then nationally, then internationally.

Beware the Pedestal

The moment you start to become 'pedestalised' and praised on a consistent basis, is the moment you need to start moving to the next level. Constantly hearing "you are amazing" and "you're doing a great job" is a great boost, but really it is mostly just massaging your ego and is the fastest way to become complacent.

Take the thanks and appreciation, be grateful for it, but acknowledge it is time to 'level up'. Remember that, when you are the smartest person in the room, you need to find a new room. You always want to keep keen, hungry, and wanting to expand your personal and business horizons. There are always new levels that you can strive towards.

In a business sense, if you are in a supportive networking group with businesses that are turning over, say £500k per year and you start to turnover £600k, £700k, they are going to look up to and congratulate you. This is when you need to move up to a networking group for businesses doing £1m, £2m (if your goal is to have a bigger business, with bigger impact that helps more people).

Also, track your numbers – not just in a business or financial sense, but if you are targeting the number of people you can impact on, performance in the sporting arena, weight loss, charitable donations raised – whatever your KPIs are for success, you need to continue to keep track and know your numbers.

Adaptability

The only constant in life is change. By being aware of existing and upcoming change, you will be able to stay ahead of the competition and spot new opportunities and also prevent slowdown.

Did you start your business by seeing an opportunity and were able to react swiftly and nimbly to offer a great product or service? Many businesses start the same way, and then as they grow and become more established, they become burdened with bureaucracy and a stifled way of thinking.

The world around us is constantly changing, and despite this there are countless examples of businesses that did not adapt to changing markets. This could be because they did not see different technologies, consumer behaviours, or opportunities coming along or were slow to respond as they had lost their ability to swiftly react to changes due to their scale.

Blockbuster vs Netflix

Blockbuster had a great international movie rental business where people would walk into a store, browse around, hire the movie for a few days, and then return it on time or face a fine.

This model worked for a long time and no doubt Blockbuster's Board of Directors felt comfortable. Then, with faster internet speeds, an opportunity was created which Netflix exploited, and Blockbuster did not.

Netflix asked itself the following questions:

- What if a customer did not have to travel into a store to hire the movie, and then have to travel back a few days later because of a deadline or worse, a fine?
- What about presenting a list of movies that they could select from the comfort of their own home and not have to worry about deadlines or fines as all they had to do was simply stream the movie via their internet?

Traditional Taxi vs Uber

Taxi drivers have had a great ride in their industry, with little changing, as what could possibly affect the need for people to travel between point A and point B?

Then Uber arrived and introduced people to the concept of on-demand transport that could be booked in advance via their mobiles easily and conveniently, rather than standing in a queue on a rainy day, hoping that a taxi might turn up.

What is interesting with Uber is that they do not own any vehicles themselves: they simply connect customers with registered drivers. The taxi industry has not reacted well to this upstart and disruptor, and has even pressured governments to stifle this innovation: a clear sign that it does not have a strong response or is able to easily adapt to this threat to their business model. It is interesting to see a "if you can't beat 'em, join 'em" response from some traditional taxi drivers who are now, either switching to driving for Uber, or signing up for new on-demand apps which are similar to Uber.

Avoiding complacency with your own success means constantly being on the lookout for weaknesses within your own business and turning them into strengths. Also look at how else you could serve your customers, use technology to become more efficient, or carve out a new niche using a combination of ideas, exploiting weaknesses in other industries with tenacity.

Think like a start-up by always looking for emerging markets and opportunities, and try not to be blinkered by early successes. Stay hungry. Also keep an eye on new technologies and consider how they might be able to help you add value.

Leaving a Legacy

At the very beginning of this book, you were asked to think big. We believe your success plan has brought great change within yours and other people's lives, but what will you leave behind for others to remember you by or to draw inspiration from?

What legacy will you leave behind? What dynasty will you begin?

It could be as small, but still significant, as having children who were brought up in a loving environment to go on and help others as well. Or maybe your success plan was as bold as being the first person to set foot on another planet? Neil Armstrong has certainly left the world and many generations an amazing and inspirational legacy.

How about building up an impressive business or investment portfolio which your descendants can grow and then leave for their descendants? There is a great sense of satisfaction when your descendants (children or business partners) have the same core values as yourself and you know they will continue the hard work you have begun.

We are on this planet for a few short years, so it is important to make the biggest and best impact possible. Why delay something that you know will benefit yourself and others? So, we ask you again: what will you leave behind?

Giving Back

One of the most rewarding things about being successful is being able to give back and help others. It could be financial assistance to a start-up, helping homeless people, or it could be offering your guidance and experiences to someone who was in a similar position to you when you first started on your success journey.

Just as people have helped you along your route to success by offering advice, support, and guidance, you should do the same. The spirit of reciprocity is a very important thing to have.

There are many ways you could help others, such as:

- You could help when asked or offer advice should you see a need for it.
- You could offer your services and be paid for it. Why not become a mentor to someone who is where you were when you started your journey?
- Could you help society and solve some of its problems? Help could come in the form of monetary donations, time, or expertise.

What greater feeling is there than helping others, seeing them grow and overcome challenges with your guidance? Maybe you could guide them through or even give them a copy of this book to help unlock their potential and achieve their own path to success – they will thank you in the long run for it.

There are often arguments about the rich being greedy or hoarding wealth, and there is a wealth disparity. However, some of the most generous people we know are wealthy individuals. By being wealthy, you have undoubtedly created a business which pays tax, and employs staff who, in turn, are able to support their families, and then also go on to pay more tax.

Bill Gates, founder of Microsoft, made billions of dollars in his lifetime. He co-founded the Bill and Melinda Gates Foundation to tackle some amazing causes, such as eradicating malaria.

Not content with this, he has encouraged other billionaires to donate substantial sums of money to help his foundation and, in turn, aid society.

What legacy will you leave, and what memories will your nearest and dearest relatives have of you when you are gone?

Summary

- Success is built on many levels and as soon as you achieve what you previously thought would be a classification of 'successful', your vision will broaden, and your goals will reset (if this hasn't already happened along the way).

- As you 'level up', retain a sense of gratitude for what you have at that present time and perspective on how far you have come. Whilst you may feel unsuccessful in achieving your new goal, remember where you started out in relation to where you are now. Balance ambition and drive with gratitude and perspective.

- Being obsessed with your success journey is great, but don't forget to have some balance and make time for experiences, and time with friends and family, as you don't want to regret not having done so as you die.

- Do not allow complacency to set in as you start to become more successful. This is the quickest route to destroying what you have created.

- Be persistent in your success journey, but know when to call it quits and reset with a new idea or business.
- Think about the legacy you want to leave the world and how you want to be remembered by those closest to you.

Action Steps

1. Write down some of the key things that have contributed towards the success you have had in the past 10 years. How will you ensure you maintain these traits and not get complacent as you grow?
2. Think about taking moments to celebrate small successes along the way, to keep yourself motivated and reward all the hard work you have put in.
3. Complete the Chapter 10 tasks in the Your Success Toolkit (available at www.yoursuccesspodcast.com/toolkit), including ways to 'level up' and look at the next stage of your success journey.

Chapter 11

Summary and Next Steps

You now have everything you need to start your success journey. The key learnings from each chapter are summarised below.

In **Chapter 1 - What is Success?** You learned that the definition of success is individual to you and how to define your vision of success. From your vision, you are now able to work out how to fulfil it and take note of the action steps to get started.

In **Chapter 2 – Motivation and Inspiration**, you learned that you need both motivation and inspiration in your life and on your journey to success. The easiest person to lie to is yourself, so find an accountability partner to keep you on track. You learned about the hyper-effective state of being in flow and how to find your flow, which can really accelerate your path to success as well as your enjoyment of the journey.

In **Chapter 3 – Constant Learning and Growth**. You learned that successful people appreciate the value of education as a way to leverage those who have already done what it is you are trying to achieve. You also learned that successful people have a growth mindset as opposed to a fixed mindset and never believe they know it all, as well as learning from failure to improve themselves going forward.

In **Chapter 4 – Determination and Perseverance**, you learned that you will face adversity on your path to success and it is your level of commitment and determination that will dictate your level of success. You learned that it is okay to have down days, but that you have to pick yourself up from these and move on. You also learned that patience is required as anything worth having takes time.

In **Chapter 5 – Ownership and Responsibility**, you learned that you must take ownership and responsibility for your life as this gives you control over your destiny. You learned to remove excuses from your vocabulary and not to live with regret.

In **Chapter 6 – Fear and Limiting Beliefs**, you learned that fear is not real but that everyone has been fearful of something at some point in their life. You learned that limiting beliefs hold you back and you learned ways to conquer these. You also learned not to be scared of getting a 'no' and how to use it to your advantage.

In **Chapter 7 – Environment**, you learned that an ability to control your environment is one of the most important success traits within environment, the people you most closely associate with will have the biggest impact on your success, in either a positive or negative way. You learned that habits and paradigms control your day to day decisions as well as how to become aware of these to change your decision-making for the better.

In **Chapter 8 – Communication**, you learned that communication, both internally and externally, is a key trait of success. You learned that building your brand is important in order to communicate effectively with people, and you also learned that empathy is a key skill to have in order to understand others and communicate more effectively with them.

In **Chapter 9 – Action**, you learned that action is one of the fundamental success traits and that no positive change occurs without a massive amount of action in line with your values and your 'why'. You learned the importance of starting now and getting perfect later, and that action is greater than talent. You also learned that your ability to say 'no' will be a key determinant of your level of success.

In **Chapter 10 – Long Term Success**, you learned that success is built in levels and that as you grow, your vision broadens and your goals reset. You learned the importance of gratitude as you level up, and also the importance of having perspective on how far you have come. You learned that obsession is a good thing in short bursts, but needs to be balanced out with periods of relaxation and/or time with friends and family. You also learned to be aware of complacency setting in and to think about the legacy you want to leave the world, and how you want to be remembered.

You have invested time and money with this book and we want you to be a success, which is why we have created the Your Success Toolkit. This complements the book very well by giving you practical tips on achieving your success.

Download for free at www.yoursuccesspodcast.com/toolkit

Your success is our success, and we would love to hear your success stories after reading this book and implementing the teachings!

To your success!

Angelos and Mo

We would very much appreciate it if you would head over to Amazon.co.uk and leave us a review on what you thought of our book. Plus, don't forget to connect with us and say 'hello'.

Your feedback is important to us and we read every message!

Email: hello@yoursuccesspodcast.com

YouTube: Your Success Podcast

Facebook: Your Success Podcast

Instagram: yoursuccesspodcast

Twitter: yoursuccesspod

Website: www.yoursuccesspodcast.com

Acknowledgements

Firstly, thank you to our parents (Panayiota and Adrian Sanders and Susan Haykir) who helped shaped us into who we are today and for their continued support.

Thank you also to our partners, Thea and Lucy who have supported us through the book writing process and have been so understanding when we've had to take ourselves away for book writing weekends, in order to fit the writing around our busy schedules.

A special thanks to our peers who took the time to review the book and gave us great feedback which has helped make the book even better. Val McKie, Peter Hill, Anthony Vasiliou, Ben Taylor, Lucy Shaffer, Rubén Tojeiro 'Senor' Gonzalez, Andy Rowell, James 'Baywatch' Fowler and Kay Taylor – you are all awesome.

Thank you to our star illustrator, Natasha Kozlova from Novorossiysk, Russia, who hand drew all of the pictures in this book and is destined to become a famous artist. Thank you to Rick McMunn for guiding us through the book writing process. Also, thank you to our editor, Jacob Senior!

A massive thank you to all of our interviewees on Your Success Podcast, as well as our listeners around the globe and of course, you the reader!

Without you, this would not have been possible. We have so much more to give you all, so stay tuned!

Testimonials

"I've travelled all over the world and met many inspirational business people and entrepreneurs from all walks of life who are doing big things – Angelos and Mo are included in that list.

They're leading the way and showing people that because of the day and age we live in, you can still make a living doing what you love, you have the power to create your own future. I love that they just get out there and do their thing."

Mark Ormrod, former Royal Marine turned entrepreneur.

"Angelos and Mo's book is a must-have resource for any aspiring or established entrepreneur. Their teaching methods are truly ground-breaking. Follow them, and you'll succeed!"

Richard McMunn, Number 1 Bestselling Author and Award-Winning Publisher.

"Success is nothing new: people have been striving for it for centuries. The two key ingredients are passion, which Angelos and Mo have in bucket loads, and to learn from the best ideas (and worst mistakes) of others. That really is the whole point of their book. Read and learn."

Peter Hill, author of *Pricing for Profit*, experienced business consultant and Chartered Accountant.

"Are you committed to creating a great life?

If the answer is yes but you are not too sure how, then this book is for you.

Working together, Angelos and Mo have created a practical blueprint for success that will support you on your journey. An inspiration and a must read for anyone looking to move forward towards success."

Val McKie M.A., B.A.(Hons), Member of the Institute of Directors, Chair of the British Acupuncture Federation International Corporate Cheerleader, Author of the soon to be released book, *Heartset: A Guide That Takes You Beyond Mindset To Unlock Your True Potential.*

"Success isn't achieved by super-humans doing extraordinary things. It's achieved by normal, everyday people like you and me. People like Angelos and Mo, who in the course of this book uncover the tell-tale signs, habits and routines of ordinary people who have succeeded. I know this book will be a success for them, and I think it will be for you too. Success leaves clues. You just need to follow them."

John Lamerton, bestselling author of *Big Ideas... for Small Businesses – Simple, Practical Tools and Tactics to Help Your Small Business Grow.*

What Success Means to You

During the course of this book, you will have discovered what success means to you and that is very important. As part of Your Success Podcast, we have interviewed many fascinating people from many different worlds and we asked them what success means to them. The following definitions of success are individual to each person and we hope you will gain some insight into their thinking and beliefs about success.

Success, for me, is that I come to work and work with clients that I like; I do work that I enjoy. I am a great believer that if you do those things, financial success will follow. So, if you're good at what you do, you enjoy what you do, and you're passionate about what you do, then the money will come in somewhere down the line.

Peter Hill, author and business consultant

Success means to me that what I achieve makes a huge difference to a lot of people, who can then also achieve success.

Andy Price, solicitor and business owner

To me, success is working in a role you enjoy, for a business you love, and alongside people who support you as much as you support them.

Katy McKenna, marketing and communications professional

Success to me means having time to do what I want, with who I want, when I want. Having spent the past nine years grafting on the business, my main goal now is to spend quality time with the people I love, whilst inspiring others to be the best they can be.

Peter Cann, chef and business owner

⋆★⋆

For me success is being able to use my experience, knowledge, and skills to increase awareness, knowledge, and professionalism within property sourcing, to such a level that we achieve 100% compliance across the whole sector and with that achievement the 'dodgy dealing' title that we currently have is a thing of the past, assuring property investors of a much more professional, legal and ethical service.

Tina Walsh, former Police Officer and property sourcing expert

⋆★⋆

Success represents what we all strive to achieve and to me it falls into the following statements:

- Having a happy and contented family life with a great work/life balance.
- Keeping the drive and enthusiasm to help others both personally and on a business basis to achieve their goals.
- To smile every day, and to always remember that there is no elevator to success; you have to take the stairs.
- To celebrate achievements with others and remember that it is amazing what can be achieved together, when nobody cares who gets the credit.
- Embrace change as it is the only constant.

David Ottley, experienced banker and business owner

Success can be fleeting and very much stop-start. Success to me means arriving at a place in my life where I can engage more on my terms, whatever they currently are or will become. I can take time to spend with family, friends, and anyone I meet who I would like to spend time with, in whatever place that is. It means taking those projects or roles that now align with my values, not with the pay check. It means being able to give back positively and making a difference in my own small way.

Peter O'Hora, property developer

Success, for me, means freedom, and that's the freedom to choose how I spend each day. Freedom to take three weeks off over Christmas and just ski and the freedom to help the causes that you want to help. I'm certainly not wealthy by any means, but I have enough now to have that freedom to choose who I want to work with, how I want to work with and a bit more on my own terms as well. And that, for me, defines success.

Nicole Bremner, author, property developer and social media expert

Success, for me, is having a balance in all areas of your life. The biggest part of success for me is being okay with you as a person. So, spiritually, mentally, physically being okay with exactly who you are. And mindset is really important. And then of course, I love cash!

Liam Ryan, property developer

To me 'Success' means being able to do what you love, when you want, with the people you want in a place of your choosing. Success is not the key to happiness; happiness is the key to success. But to do this you need to have the ability to build a successful business or businesses that make money for you without your day to day involvement. You are a long time dead so make sure you live your life to its fullest.

Alan 'Paddy' Porter, entrepreneur and property investor

⋆★⋆

Success, for me, is all about my well-being. It's all about my family life; having a good, strong family base support around me. I think that's massive – and just having my overall health. Yes, money comes with that. If you have a passion for something, eventually if you're lucky enough, something will come from that, financially.

James Jordan, personal fitness coach

⋆★⋆

Success, for me, is waking up and doing a job that I absolutely adore, growing every day and developing as a person. I think that's the main thing for me, personal growth and that translates to my work.

Andrea Vasiliou, actress

⋆★⋆

Success, for me, means that I have the ability to choose how I spend my time and who with. I've learned over the years that it's not about the material things in life, its more about experiences and who you experience that with. Therefore, that becomes a factor of time. Success is creating shared value for the people around me who I enjoy the company of, allowing me to use my time with people to the best of my ability.

Mark Stokes, author and property developer

Success, for me, means having a level of self-awareness and understanding as to what you're all about. Understanding your purpose and values sets and then going out and fulfilling them. I think lots of people, even myself in my early twenties, are driven by winning and that could be success in terms of selections or captain of England or number of victories, cash. It's all pretty shallow, hollow, and it doesn't last. The consistency is not there because it's not rooted in real purpose and real value. And real self-awareness as to why that is really important to you.

Ollie Phillips, former England Rugby 7's Captain, now business person

---

Success to me is about fulfilling my potential, so that I can ensure that my clients, family, and friends do the same. Being in the business consultant space, I read an awful lot of books. I always used to see the line "do great things for your clients and the rest will take care of itself".

This always seemed like a lovely line, but I didn't believe it; that is until after a number of years I started doing it consistently. Since that turning point, my business has grown dramatically, many of my clients are now good friends and I simply love what I do. Who wouldn't want to get out of bed in the morning to help their friends make more money, take more time away from their business, and have better experiences with their friends and family? My success comes from their success. That's what success looks and feels like to me.

Nick Jervis, author and business consultant

Success, for me, well the way I look at it, and this was penned in the 50's by a guy called Earl Nightingale, and a direct quote. "Success is a progressive realization of a worthy ideal." Well, I understand that as if you're progressively moving towards a worthy ideal, your goal, you're a successful person. If you're taking steps every single day, you're taking the knockbacks on the chin, as you will do. You will have your bad days, you'll have the losses, but you progressively move towards your worthy ideal, your goal, you're a successful person.

James Marks, personal development coach and entrepreneur

Success, for me, has got to be peace of mind. It has to be the first thing because if you don't have peace of mind, it will kill you early.

David Thomas, Guinness World Record Holder and inspirational speaker

Success, for me, is being very comfortable: not having to worry about finances and not having to worry about how I spend my time. I'm not after a mansion and a load of fast cars; it's just being comfortable. It's having the time to see my family grow up, having several streams of income and being able to manage them without it taking up all of my time.

David Aggiss, entrepreneur

Success, for me, is living life on your own terms. Doing what you want to do and being happy doing it. Having the job you want to have, making money the way you want to make it, doing podcasts or YouTubing or whatever it is you want to do, whatever you're passionate about, figure that out and make a success out of it.

Mark Ormrod, former Royal Marine turned entrepreneur.

Success, for me, is where I'm at to an extent which is not dreading coming to work but absolutely loving everything that I do that day. Some days, I don't feel successful and feel like I'm failing and not enjoying it. So, it's not about a goal for me. For some people it is, like, "I will be successful when I hit this." But for me, it's all about the journey.

Jacob Corlett, entrepreneur and founder of 'Shift'

Success to me is a sense of satisfaction in a job well delivered, and having exceeded expectations – reaching the end of the week with pride. Maintaining your integrity and having the freedom both financially and in work life balance to always be able to prioritise what is most important in life.

Clare Baker, Barclays Bank development manager

Success for me meant fulfilling the ambition that I had in my life and that was to help my parents become self-sufficient and retire them earlier than the usual retirement age. I am proud to say that I achieved this ambition for them. Shortly afterwards, I also achieved early retirement for myself by creating my various businesses. When my mother passed away, it devastated me and forced me to re-evaluate what was important in life, as my motivation for being successful had changed. Fast-forward to now, and I am pleased to see my children grow their own businesses and seeing this, makes everything worthwhile.

Taso Mavris, entrepreneur

Success, for me, well my very first definition of success in business was the very first cheque I received for my efforts. It was about £13.51. That was the moment I succeeded, because that was the moment I proved the model like "OK, this works. All I need to do is scale up. 13.51 pounds in 9 months. Can I earn 13.51 in a month? Can I earn 13.51 in a week? In a day? In an hour? In a minute?" And it was just a case of scaling up until I hit those targets. For me, that was success because just instantly, I knew that I had it within me to be in complete control of my own destiny.

John Lamerton, author and serial entrepreneur

Success, for me, is living your life by your design. I think it's as simple as that; and what lies underneath that sentence is taking responsibility. If you want to have lots of holidays, that's absolutely fine. How are you going to fund them? Create the business that will generate that income in a way that also ticks other boxes. So, creating, in my case, decent homes for decent tenants to live in, providing a good quality service, always responding to maintenance queries, not being greedy. So, you just need to create anything that you want in your life yourself by identifying the resources that are needed.

Vicki Wusche, author, property investor and entrepreneur

Success, for me, means make money, and make a difference. I think there's too much hippie shit out there at the moment which is like, "The most important thing in life is happiness." No, it isn't: because if we're all sat there in a circle singing Kumbaya feeling happy, when you're happy, you don't go out there and fix problems, you don't go out there and put yourself in an uncomfortable situation and challenge yourself to get better, to grow, to fix problems, to eat the frog, to make the hard calls whether it's customer service or sales or that big pitch that you've got and shitting your pants about. You don't do any of that when you're happy.

Rob Moore, author and serial entrepreneur

Success, for me, means being good at what you do. For me, a successful person is really good at what they're doing. It might just be a waitress in a restaurant or it might be someone at the carwash, but they're successful if they're really good at what they do and they like doing what they do. Success for me is measured in the success of my own businesses, the success of the people I'm teaching, paying it forward and making them more successful and that's where success is measured in terms of doing what you want to do with your life with the people you want to do it with.

Simon Coulson, author and serial entrepreneur

Success, for me, is the freedom I get to do whatever I want to do, and I can work as much or as little as I like. It is the freedom for me and also seeing people succeed – if I can have been a little bit of help in them achieving success in their book that is a great feeling.

Richard McMunn, author and serial entrepreneur

Success, for me, is the journey, not the destination. It's about having clarity on what you are aiming for and choosing the challenges you want to conquer in order to get there. But most importantly, it's about getting enjoyment and fulfilment from the process of getting from where you are now to where you want to be.

Jackie Tomes, property investor and mindset specialist

Success, for me, is best described by being happy in both personal and business life as they both play a part in achieving success. Sometimes you are not even aware that you are successful until others tell you so in what you have achieved Always believe in yourself and never give up!

Richard Rabin, Lettings Director

⋆★⋆

Success, for me, in business is building and running a profitable and reputable land and new homes business for Lang Town & County. From past experience I know how hard I am on myself to achieve, and I'm not sure I will ever let myself feel I have got to that point. I guess that's what drives us!

James Clarke, Land and New Homes Director

⋆★⋆

Success, for me, in a work context, I guess it would be appreciation from a client for what I have done for them. Being appreciated in both work and home life is arguably one of the most important things. I think appreciation/positive recognition that you have made a difference to someone in a beneficial/ positive way is very important and fulfilling.

Philip Oke, Legal Partner

⋆★⋆

Success, for me, means enjoying every day of my life. On that theme, I am very successful thanks to having a lovely family, great colleagues. and excellent business relationships.

Gordon McCaw, tax advisor specialist

Success, for me, is living life to the full, from a space of love and belonging. Being at ease with ourselves and our lives. Sharing wisdom, knowledge and insights to help make the world a better place. Being able to view everything that happens as part of a longer term deeper force for good.

Val McKie, author and personal development expert

Success is the realisation that you can never be completely successful. Whatever you've done, you could always have done and achieved more. It is that simple realisation that brings true success – because next time, if you learn, you will achieve more and, with experience, become even more successful. Complacency is the enemy of success.

James Barron, business owner

Success, for me, means waking up and knowing the world is full of opportunities that I can explore.

Angelos Sanders, author, public speaker, and entrepreneur

Success, for me, means growing everyday and developing as a person, and also having freedom to choose how I spend my time.

Mo Haykir, author, public speaker, and entrepreneur

Success, for me, is achieving my goals, both in my professional and personal life without deviating from my core values.

James Yorke, property developer and entrepreneur

Success, for us, means when you change the way you look at things, the things you look at change. If you choose to label something as a problem, you will give it the energy to be a problem, which means you give it the power to limit you. The only thing that limits you is you!

Jo Eva and Maz Berry, personal development coaches

⋆★⋆

Success, for me, is achieving your goals without compromising your integrity, honesty, or beliefs and not just valuing your customers, but being valued by them.

Daniel Lampard, Ocean BMW business development manager

⋆★⋆

Success, for me, is the health of my family, plus being in a position where income exceeds expenses.

Philip Bailey, property developer and entrepreneur

36672863R00120

Printed in Great Britain
by Amazon